# Creative
# Monthly Calendars

# Creative MONTHLY CALENDARS

## 24 Theme-Based Calendars for Students to Make and Take

by Tracy Jarboe and Stefani Sadler

## Crystal Springs BOOKS

A Division of Staff Development for Educators (SDE)

Peterborough, New Hampshire

Published by: Crystal Springs Books
A division of Staff Development for Educators
10 Sharon Road, PO Box 500
Peterborough, NH 03458
1-800-321-0401
www.crystalsprings.com
www.sde.com

© 2003 Tracy Jarboe and Stefani Sadler
Published 2003
Printed in the United States of America
07 06      3 4 5

ISBN-13: 978-1-884548-55-0
ISBN-10: 1-884548-55-5

**Library of Congress Cataloging-in-Publication Data**

Jarboe, Tracy, 1964-
  Creative monthly calendars : 24 theme-based calendars for students to
make and take / by Tracy Jarboe and Stefani Sadler.
       p. cm.
  ISBN 1-884548-55-5
  1.  Creative activities and seat work. 2.  Unit method of teaching. 3.
Calendars.  I. Sadler, Stefani, 1951- II. Title.
LB1027.25.J37 2004
372.5—dc22
                        2003021384

Editor: Meredith A. Reed O'Donnell
Art Director and Production Coordinator: Soosen Dunholter
Illustrator: Stefani Sadler

# Dedication

For my big sister Shallie, who is my best friend every day of the year! *Tracy*

To my family, for keeping my calendar filled with fun. *Stefani*

# About the Authors

Tracy Jarboe and Stefani Sadler have more than 25 years' combined teaching experience in the primary classroom. Tracy has a B.A. in child psychology, a multiple subjects credential, and a CLAD credential; she is working on a masters in administration and educational leadership. She has been nominated for Disney's American Teacher Award. Stefani has a B.A. in graphic arts communications and a multiple subjects credential with supplementary authorization in music and art; she also has an M.A. in curriculum and instruction.

Both Tracy and Stefani are respected national presenters and authors, and Stefani is also a successful illustrator. Tracy and Stefani's varied experiences within the world of education include serving as kindergarten, math, and integrated arts mentors; functioning as BTSA support providers and trainers; and working as primary lead and ELL teachers.

Tracy and Stefani currently reside in San Diego, California—Tracy with her husband, two children, and their assortment of beloved pets; Stefani with the youngest of her four children and their assortment of beloved pets. Tracy and Stefani are the authors of *It's As Easy As ABC*.

# Contents

## Monthly Themes

### January

### February

### March

### April

### May

# June

# July

# August

# September

# October

# November

# December

# Appendix

# Introduction

*Creative Monthly Calendars* is an effective instructional tool designed to teach and reinforce these and other developmentally appropriate learning concepts:

- number sense
- measurement
- geometry
- analysis
- reasoning
- word sense
- fine motor skill development

Monthly calendar units contain two different themes for teachers to choose from, allowing educators the opportunity to select the most appropriate theme for her/his classroom. Each calendar and theme component is designed to complement and enhance current curriculum and instruction, offering students optimal learning opportunities that span the curriculum. Best of all, components are easily adaptable to fit any instructional program.

Included in *Creative Monthly Calendars* are all the components teachers will need to complete a year of monthly themed calendars. These include:

- literature suggestions to start each theme unit
- activities
- reproducible calendar-art patterns and instructions
- reproducible poem pages

Theme-unit activities teachers do not select for the entire class may be used for independent study in math, art, and/or literacy. The authors have also included a "Fun Celebrations" page at the end of each month for those teachers interested in acknowledging additional noteworthy dates and themes.

Teachers, parents, and students alike will find *Creative Monthly Calendars* innovative and fun. Students will take pride in sharing each finished calendar with those they love.

# How to Use This Book

Each month is divided into two separate themes; choose the theme most appropriate for your classroom. Jumpstart each theme unit by reading one or more of the suggested book titles; follow by reading the corresponding poem/finger-play. With your students construct individual calendars according to the specified directions, and if time permits, engage students in one or more of the suggested activities throughout the month.

The beauty of this program lies in its flexibility—there is no "one way" to progress through a theme. For example, in our classrooms, we begin a theme unit by reading the theme poem in the morning. Later in the day (our designated "calendar time") we introduce the calendar art activity by reading one of the stories. During calendar time the remainder of the week we read another book and engage in one of the suggested activities. Every teacher approaches calendar time differently, however, so feel free to experiment to find out what schedule works best for you and your class.

Before the month begins, create a larger version of the calendar students will be making and taking home individually. Tack or staple this calendar to a bulletin board. Your class will now be able to interact with the calendar for the entire month.

Following is a more detailed description of each theme component.

**Literature Link:** Introduce each month by reading one or more of the literature suggestions listed at the beginning of each theme unit. The titles are well-known and, along with the theme's corresponding poem, are sure to excite students and encourage discussion. Feel free to share titles of your own choosing, too.

**Poems and Poem Finger-Plays:** Each theme unit includes a poem or finger-play for students to practice and learn. Use these selections to teach such concepts as rhyme, word patterns, sight words, and letter sense. (Finger-plays are poems or rhymes you can dramatize using hand motions or puppets.) You can use the verse separately, transfer it to sentence strips for pocket chart activities, and/or attach it to the calendar itself. By attaching it to the calendar, children are able to share and revisit it at home with their parents. Simply reproduce the words on a piece of white paper or a piece of colored paper (Xerox paper or, if your photocopier permits, construction paper) that complements the calendar art. We have included four or more poem boxes per sheet, to save you time at the photocopier; the poem box size is the appropriate size for the calendar. Teachers, be sure to practice each poem/finger-play before reading it out loud to your class.

**Activities:** The activities included will extend learning across the curriculum. Use these activities in connection with the creation of the actual calendars, or introduce them during other instructional times for whole-group or independent exercises. We have grouped together skills by code for those activities included within a particular theme. Please refer to the skills chart on page 19 for the names of individual skills for each activity. It is not necessary to engage in every activity.

**The Calendar (overview):** Each theme unit comes with patterns and detailed, step-by-step instructions on how to create a calendar that is both attractive and instructive. Once students have completed their individual calendars at the beginning of the month, they can bring them home to share (and admire!) with their parents. Suggest to students they use their calendars to record the weather, holidays, family activities, or other significant events for that month. (For those months school is not in session, you might consider sending the calendars home as independent work.)

**Creating the Calendar:** Each theme unit includes step-by-step instructions on how to prepare and place the various calendar components on the construction paper background. Unless the age or ability of your students dictates otherwise, allow your students to cut out individual pattern pieces themselves. For guidance on how to position each component, be sure to refer to the sample calendar located in the lower right-hand corner of each "Create the Calendar" page.

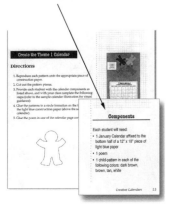

Although creating the calendar is really quite simple, you might consider preparing calendar components beforehand. For example, you could construct the "skeleton" calendar by attaching the calendar month to the appropriate background color (see individual themes for suggested background colors). To do this, simply glue or staple the correct calendar to the bottom portion of a twelve-by-eighteen piece of construction paper for each calendar art project.

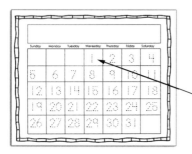

**Calendar Grids:** In the appendix (pages 185–196) you will find seven reproducible calendar grids with dotted numbers for students to trace. Choose the grid that displays the weekday on which the first day of that month falls. For example, if January starts on a Wednesday this particular school year, find the calendar option on which the first day of the month (January) appears underneath Wednesday.

Each calendar page contains the numbers 1–31. Cover the dates you will not use with white Post-it tape before photocopying. For example, for your February calendar you will need to cover the numbers 29–31 before photocopying the calendar page, as there are only 28 days in the month (with the exception of leap year). A blank calendar has also been included for students who are ready to print the dates independently.

In the appendix, you will also find three reproducible pages containing the names of the different months. Photocopy each month's name and attach it to the top of the appropriate calendar before photocopying for your entire class. Students who are ready can write the name of the month on the calendar independently.

**Fun Celebrations:** A "Fun Celebrations" page follows each month's theme set, and includes additional holidays, birthdays, and other familiar and unfamiliar events. Acknowledge these dates on your calendars with stickers or stamps, or celebrate with a mini-lesson, theme-based party, or activity. For more information on significant dates, try these resources:

- *Calendar Plan Book*
    by Teacher Created Materials
- *Teacher's Planbook and Calendar of Year-Round Activities*
    by Alice Bernstein and Dorothy Douglas
- *The Teacher's Calendar*
    by Sandra Whiteley and Sandy Whiteley

# General Calendar Activities

When introducing a new calendar to the students, focus on one or more of the following teaching points.

• "Let's look at the name of the month together. How many letters do you see? Let's count them together. What are the names of the letters? Wonderful! Now let's try to blend the sounds of the letters together. What is the name of the month? You're right! Now let's say that together. Let's say it again and clap the syllables as we say it. How many syllables did you hear?"

• "How many days are in one week? Which is the first day of the week? Second? Third? What two days are considered weekend days? What day is it today? Can you point to that day on your calendar?"

• "What do the numbers in the calendar grid boxes tell us? That's right! They tell us the date. How many days are in this month? What day of the week is the first day of the month? What day is the last day of the month? What is today's date? Now use your pencil to trace over the numbers. Will we start at the bottom or at the top of the number to begin tracing?" Depending on students' ability levels, you might want them to write the numbers independently.

• Be sure to highlight special events on your class and students' individual calendars. For example, place a heart around February 14 in honor of Valentine's Day or draw a shamrock around March 17 for St. Patrick's Day. Place a sticker on a date to indicate a field trip or a student's birthday. Children enjoy looking forward to each month's special events. Consider making a class graph or paper chain to count down the days to selected dates.

• Reinforce the concept of patterning by asking each student to color or outline a date box with crayon. In October you could outline the date boxes in black/orange/black/orange/black/orange, and in December try red/green/blue/red/green/blue. Make a different pattern for each month of the year. An additional concept extension involves having students trace all the odd numbers in one color and all the even numbers in a different color. The ways in which you can extend your calendar activities are endless. Have fun, and be creative!

# Additional Calendar Activities

The poems included with each theme may be used in your classroom every day in a variety of ways. Simply feature a new poem every month; write each line from the poem on individual sentence strips; then place these strips in a pocket chart. Each day read the poem with the students and complete one of the following poetry activities.

### Print Track

Thematic pointers are magical to children and make tracking print a special, highly anticipated privilege. Using a special pointer, invite different students to track the print as the class recites the poem or rhyme.

### Word Count

Give each student edible manipulatives such as Goldfish or Cheerios in snack-size Ziploc bags. Write each child's name on her/his individual bag using permanent maker or an adhesive label so students can reuse their bags in the future. For each word you say, direct students to take out one Goldfish. (Remember to say each word slowly.) When you have finished, have your students count the Goldfish to determine how many words were in the poem or rhyme. Of course, the best part is eating the counters!

You might also invite a child to come up to the pocket chart and choose a special pointer to count the words in the poem. Have the remainder of the class clap and count along.

### Choral-Read

Divide students into different groups. Groupings might include: boys/girls, rows/tables, or left/right side of the room. Invite students to choral-read the poem, with each group reading in a different voice. For example, row one might read the poem using a whisper voice, row two a loud monster voice, row three a southern accent, and row four and operatic singing voice. Or you might invite your students to read the poem using rabbit talk (fast) or turtle talk (slow). The possibilities are endless . . . and fun. Enjoy!

## Letter, Sound, and Punctuation Mark Recognition

Have your students use Wikki Stix, highlighting tape, or a finger pointer to find:

- a particular letter of the alphabet, a capital letter, a lowercase letter

- the letter that makes a specific sound

- a particular punctuation mark (Be sure to ask, "What's its job?")

## Concept Integration

Emphasize any cross-curricular concepts such as number words, color words, or science vocabulary. If you are focusing on a particular high frequency word, for example, invite the students to clap every time you come to that word. Or if you are learning number words and the poem you are reading uses number words, encourage students to highlight each number word in the poem. Highlighting can be done using highlighting tape or Wikki Stix.

## Word Match

From selected poems, copy key words onto sentence cards. Place these cards next to the pocket chart containing the poem. When reading a poem, have students match each word to the words in the poem. For young learners you may wish to add pictures to the word cards for clarification.

## Word Order

Take the words or sentence strips from the poem off the pocket chart and mix them up. Ask your students to put them back in the correct order.

## Kinesthetic Learning

Create different movements to go along with the poem or rhyme. Teach these movements and invite the children to "act out" the rhyme or poem. Consider buying or making props to go along with these dramatizations.

You can also use movements to teach punctuation:

- Reach your hands high in the air each time you come to a capital letter.

- Place a hand out to indicate STOP when you reach a period.

- Wave your hands in the air when you reach an exclamation point.

- Make quotation marks with your fingers when you see them in the poem.

- Shrug your shoulders when you come to a question mark.

- Take a deep breath each time you come to a comma.

- Try clapping the syllables of the words you read. Which words have the most syllables?

## Punctuation Check

Enlarge poems. Tape one poem at a time to the whiteboard or include as a page in a poetry big book as you introduce a new poem to your students each month. Place a sheet of acetate or clear laminate over the poem and use a dry-erase marker to do any of the following:

- Place a red circle around a capital letter.

- Place a green line underneath each rhyming word.

- Place a purple triangle around the punctuation mark that denotes excitement (exclamation point).

- Place a yellow rectangle around the punctuation mark that denotes a question (question mark).

- Locate, then circle all the capital and lowercase letter m's (or another letter of your choosing).

Continue on in this manner, focusing on current teaching concepts.

## Rhyme

Have students point out the rhyming words in the poem. Put these words up on a whiteboard. Ask your class to share other words that have the same rhyme. Write the words below the initial rhyming words and discuss the rhyme pattern.

Questions to Consider:

- In what way are these words similar?

- How are they different?

- Can you find a word that begins with a digraph?

- Can you find the common word family?

- Do all the words have the same number of letters? Determine by counting. Sort and graph.

- Do these words use a short or long vowel sound?

Jack and Jill went
up the hill.

**Rhyming Words**

| Jill | hill | Bill |
|------|-------|------|
| will | still | gill |
| drill | spill | mill |
| chill | thrill | |

Put these words on flashcards using onset and rime. Blend and segment the words verbally.

## Make New Words

With your class, determine how many smaller words you can make using the letters you find in one of the words from the poem. List these words on a whiteboard or paper chart.

| Leprechauns | |
|---|---|
| a | pal |
| see | leap |
| peach | cheap |
| speech | |
| each | |
| sun | |

## Cover the Word

After having placed the poem on sentence strips and into a pocket chart, use a piece of cardboard to cover one of the words in the pocket chart. It is best to cover a word that your students are less familiar with, in order to build vocabulary. Ask students which word is missing. Slowly reveal the letters in the word one at a time as clues.

In my garden there is a [          ]

Write responses on the board or on chart paper: friend, flower, pet, rock, etc.

Reveal clue: In my garden there is a r [          ]

"What can it be? It begins with the /r/ sound." Erase the responses that are no longer appropriate. Write the new responses on the board or chart paper: rabbit, rat, rose, raddish, rake, etc.

Continue until the word is guessed and uncovered: rainbow.

# Calendar Songs

You may wish to sing your favorite "days of the week" song to help reinforce this concept, or use one of the chants we have provided.

**Days of the Week**

Sung to the tune of "Oh My Darling Clementine"

There are seven days,
There are seven days,
There are seven days in one week:

Sunday, Monday,
Tuesday, Wednesday,
Thursday, Friday, Saturday.

**Date Song**

Sung to the tune of "Frère Jacques"

**T**eacher sings: Today is Monday, (or whichever day of the week it is)

**S**tudents repeat: Today is Monday,

**T:** September 1st,
**S:** September 1st,
**T:** 2003. (or whatever year it is)
**S:** 2003.
**T:** This is the date.
**S:** This is the date.

**Days of the Week Chant**

Sunday is the first day. (Hold up one finger.)
Monday is the second day. (Hold up two fingers.)
Tuesday is the third day of the week. (Hold up three fingers.)
Wednesday is the fourth day. (Hold up four fingers.)
Thursday is the fifth day. (Hold up five fingers.)
Friday is the sixth day of the week. (Hold up six fingers.)
Saturday is the seventh day. (Hold up seven fingers.)
It's a really fun day. (Hold hands high over head and shake them.)
Saturday is the seventh day of the week. (Make the baseball sign for "safe.")
Days of the week.
Days of the week.
There are seven days of the week.

## Codes and Skills*

| Code | Skill |
|---|---|
| A | Left-to-Right/Top-to-Bottom Progression |
| B | Comparing & Sorting Sets of Objects |
| C | Printing, Counting, & Ordering Numbers |
| D | Addition & Subtraction |
| E | Estimation |
| F | Shape & Color |
| G | Size & Position |
| H | Measurement & Graphing |
| I | Concepts of Time |
| J | Data Analysis |
| K | Patterning |

| Month | Theme | A | B | C | D | E | F | G | H | I | J | K |
|---|---|---|---|---|---|---|---|---|---|---|---|---|
| Jan. | Martin Luther King Day | • | | • | | | | | | • | | • |
| Jan. | Snowmen | • | | • | | | | • | | • | | |
| Feb. | Presidents' Day | • | • | • | | | | | | • | • | • |
| Feb. | Valentine's Day | • | • | • | | • | | | • | • | • | |
| March | Kites | • | | • | | | • | • | | • | | • |
| March | St. Patrick's Day | • | • | • | • | | | | | • | | |
| April | Baby Rabbits | • | • | • | • | | | | | • | | |
| April | April Showers | • | | • | | | | | | • | | |
| May | Mother's Day | • | | • | | | • | • | | • | | • |
| May | Flowers | • | • | • | | | | | | • | | • |
| June | Father's Day | • | | • | | | | | • | • | | |
| June | School is Out | • | | • | | | | • | | • | | |
| July | The Fourth of July | • | | • | | | | | | • | • | |
| July | At the Beach | • | | • | • | | | | | • | | • |
| Aug. | Summer Sun | • | | • | | | | | | • | | |
| Aug. | Picnic | • | | • | • | | | | | • | | |
| Sept. | Back to School | • | | • | | | • | | | • | | |
| Sept. | Apples | • | | • | | • | • | | • | • | • | |
| Oct. | Halloween | • | • | • | | | | | | • | | • |
| Oct. | Fall Leaves | • | • | • | | | • | • | | • | | |
| Nov. | Thanksgiving | • | • | • | | | | | • | • | • | |
| Nov. | Harvest | • | | • | | • | | | • | • | • | |
| Dec. | Gingerbread | • | | • | • | | • | | | • | • | |
| Dec. | Gift-Giving | • | | • | | • | | • | | • | • | |

*Located under the skills heading on each theme's opening page you will see a letter code that corresponds to a particular skill listed above.

Creative Monthly Calendars   19

# January

## Theme 1:
## Dr. Martin Luther King Day

## Theme 2:
## Snowmen

# Literature LINK

- *A Picture Book of Martin Luther King Jr.* by David A. Adler
- *What Is Martin Luther King Jr. Day?* by Margaret Friskey
- *Martin Luther King Jr. Day: Honoring a Man of Peace* by Carol Gnojewski
- *Martin Luther King Jr.: A Photograph Illustrated Biography* by Kathy Feeney

## Dr. Martin Luther King

Martin Luther King had a dream;
It's one that we all share:
To show our love, and patience too,
For people everywhere.

No matter how we live or look,
Now matter what we wear,
People are alike all over the world,
With kindness, we show we care.

## ACTIVITIES ➤

### SKILL CODES
### A, C, I, K

# Patterns of People

- Reproduce the child-pattern onto several different colors of skin-toned construction paper (approximately 12 of each color, although the number depends on how many students are working on this activity at one time). A pattern sequence must repeat itself at least three times to be considered a pattern.
- Cut the child-patterns out and laminate.
- Create patterns using the laminated child pieces. Begin with a simple ABABAB pattern and then progress to more complex patterns as students demonstrate readiness.
- Place these laminated child-patterns into an envelope or storage bin to use again in future years.

## Our Class

- Reproduce a child-pattern for each student in the class.

- Using yarn, fabric, or paper scraps, have students decorate the child cut-out to look like themselves.

- Place the finished products together on a bulletin board with a caption such as: "A Community of Learners."

## Create the Calendar

## Directions

1. Reproduce each pattern onto the suggested paper (see "Calendar Components").

2. Provide each student with the calendar components, and with your class complete the following steps:

3. Cut out the pattern pieces.

4. Glue the patterns in a circle formation on the top half of the light-blue construction paper (above the actual calendar).

5. Glue the poem in an open spot above the fold.

## Calendar Components

### Each student will need:

- 1 January Calendar affixed to the bottom half of a 12" x 18" piece of light-blue paper

- 1 poem

- 1 child-pattern in each of the following colors: dark brown, brown, tan, white

## Dr. Martin Luther King

Martin Luther King had a dream;
It's one that we all share:
To show our love, and patience too,
For people everywhere.

No matter how we live or look,
No matter what we wear,
People are alike all over the world,
With kindness, we show we care.

## Dr. Martin Luther King

Martin Luther King had a dream;
It's one that we all share:
To show our love, and patience too,
For people everywhere.

No matter how we live or look,
No matter what we wear,
People are alike all over the world,
With kindness, we show we care.

## Dr. Martin Luther King

Martin Luther King had a dream;
It's one that we all share:
To show our love, and patience too,
For people everywhere.

No matter how we live or look,
No matter what we wear,
People are alike all over the world,
With kindness, we show we care.

## Dr. Martin Luther King

Martin Luther King had a dream;
It's one that we all share:
To show our love, and patience too,
For people everywhere.

No matter how we live or look,
No matter what we wear,
People are alike all over the world,
With kindness, we show we care.

## Dr. Martin Luther King

Martin Luther King had a dream;
It's one that we all share:
To show our love, and patience too,
For people everywhere.

No matter how we live or look,
No matter what we wear,
People are alike all over the world,
With kindness, we show we care.

## Dr. Martin Luther King

Martin Luther King had a dream;
It's one that we all share:
To show our love, and patience too,
For people everywhere.

No matter how we live or look,
No matter what we wear,
People are alike all over the world,
With kindness, we show we care.

— Reproducible Page —

**Child-Pattern**

# Literature LINK

- *Snowballs* by Lois Ehlert
- *Snow Family* by Daniel Kirk
- *Snowmen at Night* by Caralyn Buehner
- *All You Need for a Snowman* by Alice Schertle

## Four Snowmen*

Looking out my window I can see
Four jolly snowmen looking at me.

The first wears a top hat, black and tall;
The second wears a cap with a fuzzy ball;
The third wears a striped hat, white and red;
The fourth wears a cowboy hat on his head.

The sun sinks down and the moon shines bright,
And four jolly snowmen say, "Goodnight!"

## ACTIVITIES ➤

### SKILL CODES

## A, C, G, I

# Flashcards

- Photocopy the melting snowman sequence pattern onto heavy construction paper or card stock. Enlarge if desired. Vary the difficulty by using three to six cards, depending on the grade level.
- Cut the snowmen into rectangular cards and laminate. You should have a total of six snowmen.
- Shuffle the cards and have your students place the cards in sequential order based on the melting stage.
- Ask your students to tell you what happened first, second, third, and so on.

# Build a Snowman

- Cut out a variety of snowman components from construction paper, including a small, medium, and large white snowball, a top hat, a baseball cap, a cowboy hat, a wig, different colored eyes, buttons, noses, and any other articles you choose. The reproducible page provides these pieces, or feel free to create your own.

*Finger-Play

- Laminate all the pieces and place them in a storage tub.
- As a "choosing activity," allow students to create snowmen using the components in the tub.

## Create the Calendar

# Directions

1. Reproduce each pattern onto the suggested paper (see "Calendar Components"). Have students complete the following steps:

2. Color each snowman according to the poem.

3. Cut out and then glue each snowman in sequence on the top half of the dark-blue construction paper (above the calendar).

4. Glue the poem in the upper left-hand corner.

5. Optional: Use a cotton ball to dab thickened white paint beneath the snowmen to look like snow. Refer to the sample calendar for visual guidance.

## Calendar Components

### Each student will need:

- 1 January Calendar affixed to the bottom half of a 12" x 18" piece of dark-blue construction paper

- 1 poem

- 1 of each snowman (reproduce on white paper)

## Four Snowmen

Looking out my window I can see
Four jolly snowmen looking at me.

The first wears a top hat, black and tall;
The second wears a cap with a fuzzy ball;
The third wears a striped hat, white and red;
The fourth wears a cowboy hat on his head.

The sun sinks down and the moon shines
bright,
And four jolly snowmen say, "Goodnight!"

## Four Snowmen

Looking out my window I can see
Four jolly snowmen looking at me.

The first wears a top hat, black and tall;
The second wears a cap with a fuzzy ball;
The third wears a striped hat, white and red;
The fourth wears a cowboy hat on his head.

The sun sinks down and the moon shines
bright,
And four jolly snowmen say, "Goodnight!"

## Four Snowmen

Looking out my window I can see
Four jolly snowmen looking at me.

The first wears a top hat, black and tall;
The second wears a cap with a fuzzy ball;
The third wears a striped hat, white and red;
The fourth wears a cowboy hat on his head.

The sun sinks down and the moon shines
bright,
And four jolly snowmen say, "Goodnight!"

## Four Snowmen

Looking out my window I can see
Four jolly snowmen looking at me.

The first wears a top hat, black and tall;
The second wears a cap with a fuzzy ball;
The third wears a striped hat, white and red;
The fourth wears a cowboy hat on his head.

The sun sinks down and the moon shines
bright,
And four jolly snowmen say, "Goodnight!"

## Four Snowmen

Looking out my window I can see
Four jolly snowmen looking at me.

The first wears a top hat, black and tall;
The second wears a cap with a fuzzy ball;
The third wears a striped hat, white and red;
The fourth wears a cowboy hat on his head.

The sun sinks down and the moon shines
bright,
And four jolly snowmen say, "Goodnight!"

## Four Snowmen

Looking out my window I can see
Four jolly snowmen looking at me.

The first wears a top hat, black and tall;
The second wears a cap with a fuzzy ball;
The third wears a striped hat, white and red;
The fourth wears a cowboy hat on his head.

The sun sinks down and the moon shines
bright,
And four jolly snowmen say, "Goodnight!"

## Snowman Patterns

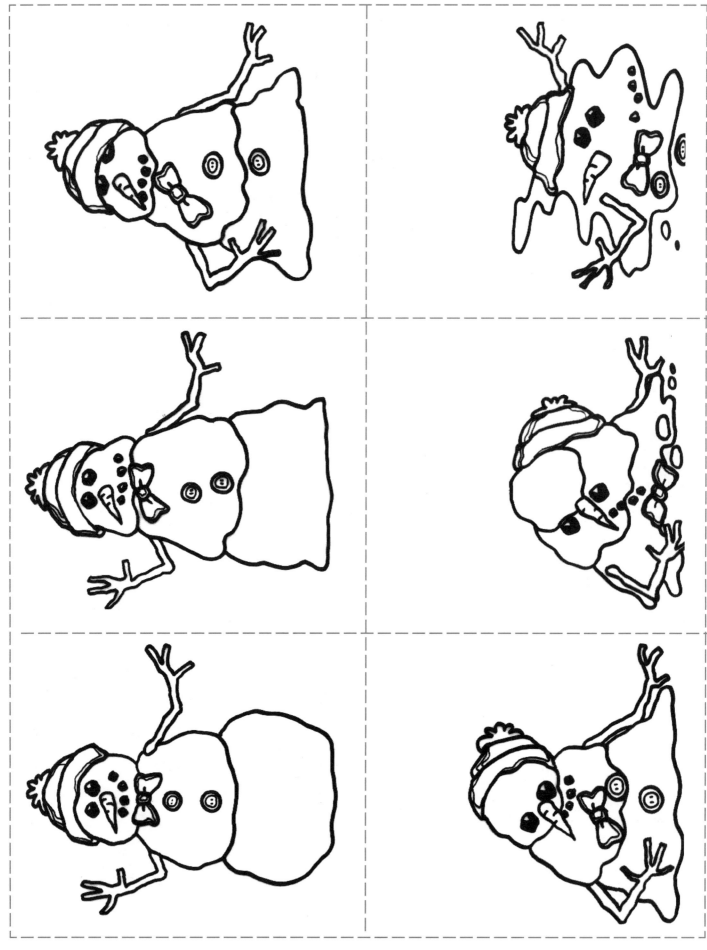

# Flashcard Patterns

— Reproducible  Page —

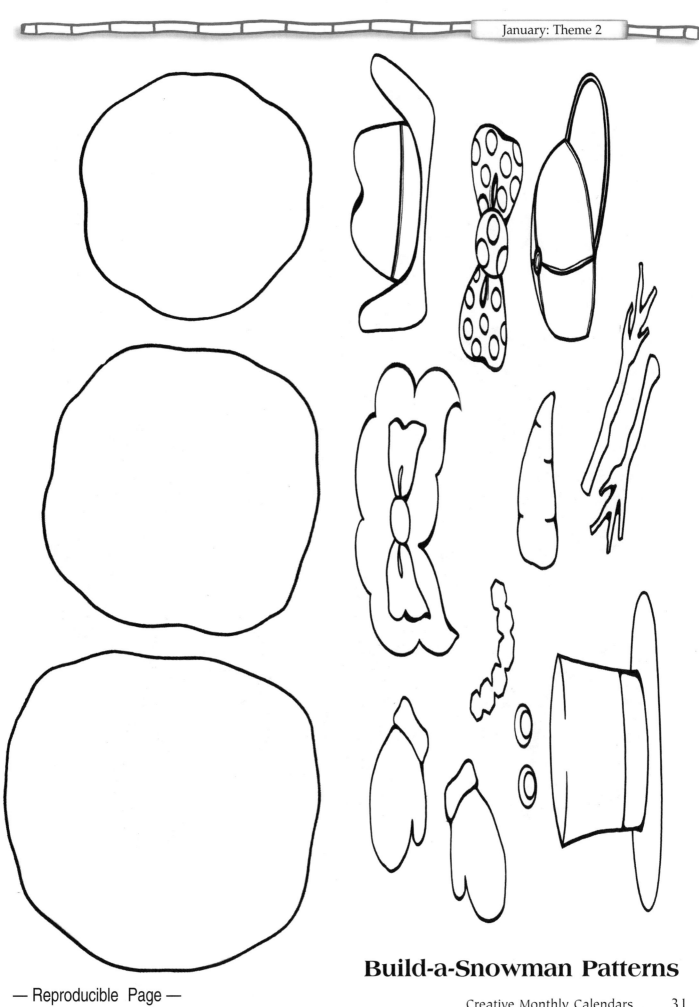

# Build-a-Snowman Patterns

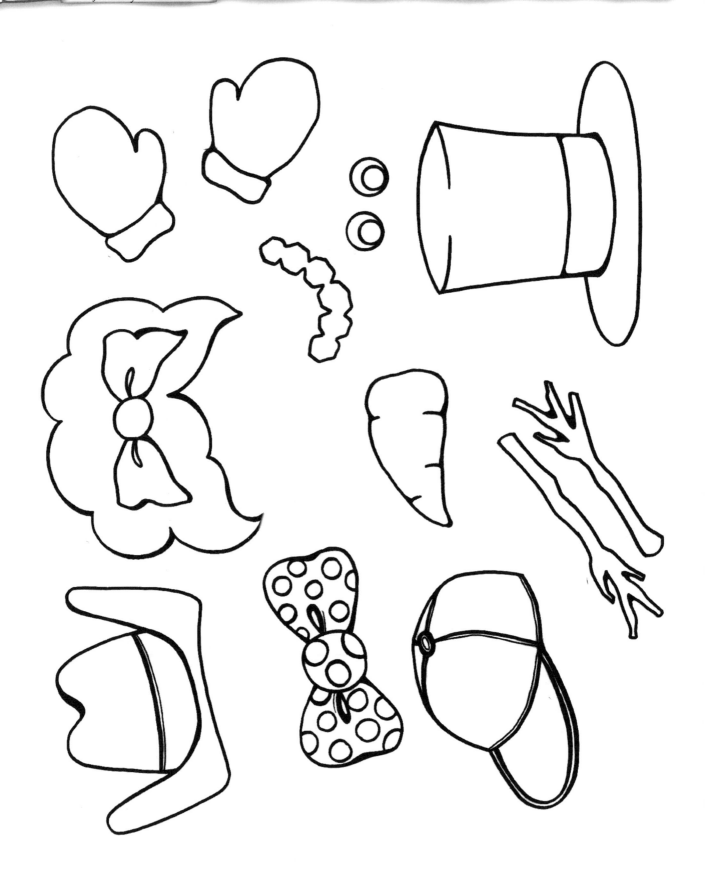

# Snowman Outfit Patterns

— Reproducible Page —

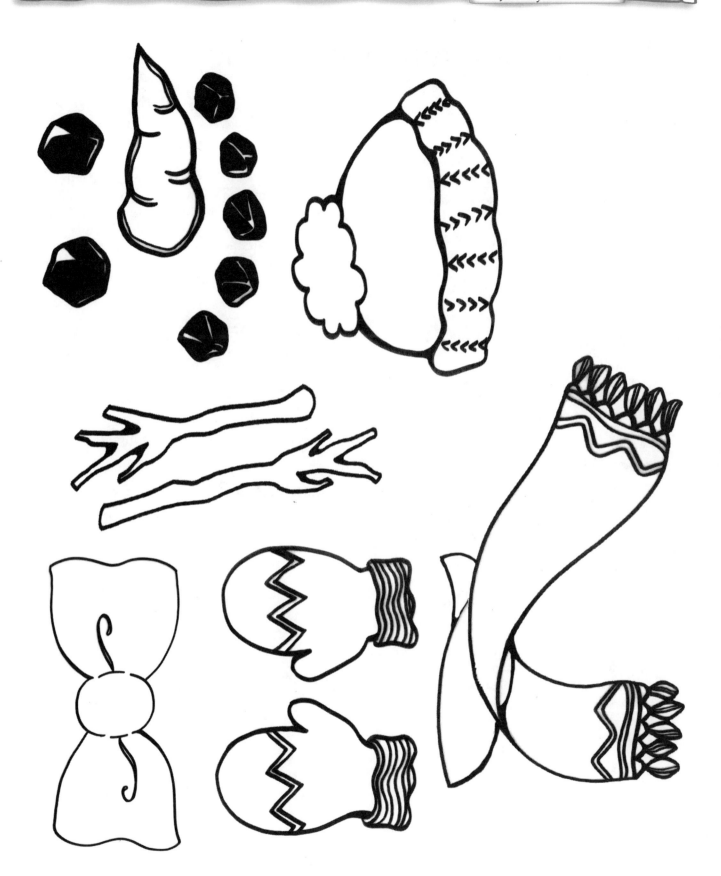

## Snowman Outfit Patterns

# Fun Celebrations for January

## January 1

- Discuss the concept of New Year's resolutions. Have each child talk or write about her/his resolution for the new year.

- Did you know that Paul Revere and Betsy Ross were born on this day?

- Today is also the anniversary of Abraham Lincoln's Emancipation Proclamation, which led to the end of slavery in the United States.

## January 15

Today is Dr. Martin Luther King Jr.'s birthday. Read his famous speech, "I Have a Dream," and ask each student to write about her/his dream for the world.

## January 18

Happy Birthday, A.A. Milne! Celebrate this day by having each student bring a teddy bear to school (bring in a few extra bears for those students who might not have one at home). Read Winnie the Pooh stories together.

## January 21

Today is National Hugging Day. Sing Charlotte Diamond's song, "Four Hugs a Day," and be sure to hug someone special!

## January 22

Today is National Compliment Day and National School Nurses Day. Pay your school nurse a compliment by letting her/him, know how much you appreciate her/him. You might want to shower the nurse with school-made cards. You might also write the definition of "compliment" on the chalkboard. Ask students to share compliments about one another.

## January 27

Happy Birthday to Wolfgang Amadeus Mozart. Celebrate this day by listening to some of the beautiful music Mozart composed, including: *Marriage of Figaro*, *Don Giovanni*, and *The Magic Flute*. Consider studying a different composer each month.

## January 31

Today is Denise Fleming's birthday. Denise Fleming is a popular illustrator best known for her work on such children's literature books as *Mama Cat Has Three Kittens*; *In the Small Pond*; and *In the Tall, Tall Grass*. Read her books today or visit her web site at www.denisefleming.com.

# February

## Theme 1:
## Presidents' Day

## Theme 2:
## Valentine's Day

# Literature LINK

- *Presidents' Day* by Amy Margaret
- *A Picture Book of George Washington* by David A. Adler
- *A Picture Book of Abraham Lincoln* by David A. Adler
- *Abe Lincoln Remembers* by Ann Warren Turner

## Washington and Lincoln

In February we celebrate
Two men who made our country great.
As presidents each led the way,
And we remember to this day
They worked for freedom and liberty,
They built America for you and me.

## ACTIVITIES ➤

### SKILL CODES

### A, B, C, I, J, K

## Penny Observation

- Give each child a penny.
- Ask each child to look at her/his penny very carefully. Look for special marks or interesting characteristics.
- Ask students: "Is your penny tarnished? What date appears on your penny? Are there any chips or scratches?"
- Discuss the characteristics of each penny.
- Place the pennies in a pile and see if each child can find her/his penny again. This activity works best if done in small groups first.

## Coin Comparison/Contrast

- Compare and contrast the characteristics of pennies and quarters.
- Ask students: "Can you tell which one has Abraham Lincoln on it and which one has George Washington on it?"

# Penny Polish

- Place a few pennies in a quarter cup of vinegar with one teaspoon of salt. What happens to the pennies? They become shiny and look like new!

## Create the Calendar

## Directions

1. Reproduce each pattern onto the suggested paper (see "Calendar Components").

2. Provide each student with the calendar components, and with your class complete the following steps:

3. Cut out the silhouettes of George Washington and Abraham Lincoln.

4. Glue the red and white squares along each side of the calendar. Create a pattern (red, white, red, white. . . .)

5. Glue the two silhouettes (so they face one another) in the center of the paper, but be sure to leave enough room to place the poem at the top center of the paper.

## Calendar Components

### Each student will need:

- 1 February Calendar affixed to the bottom half of a 12" x 18" piece of bright-blue construction paper

- 1 poem

- 1" x 1" square pieces of red and white paper: Each student needs 9 of each color

- 1 silhouette of George Washington; 1 silhouette of Abraham Lincoln (reproduce on light-blue paper)

## Washington and Lincoln

In February we celebrate
Two men who made our country great.
As presidents each led the way,
And we remember to this day
They worked for freedom and liberty,
They built America for you and me.

## Washington and Lincoln

In February we celebrate
Two men who made our country great.
As presidents each led the way,
And we remember to this day
They worked for freedom and liberty,
They built America for you and me.

## Washington and Lincoln

In February we celebrate
Two men who made our country great.
As presidents each led the way,
And we remember to this day
They worked for freedom and liberty,
They built America for you and me.

## Washington and Lincoln

In February we celebrate
Two men who made our country great.
As presidents each led the way,
And we remember to this day
They worked for freedom and liberty,
They built America for you and me.

## Washington and Lincoln

In February we celebrate
Two men who made our country great.
As presidents each led the way,
And we remember to this day
They worked for freedom and liberty,
They built America for you and me.

## Washington and Lincoln

In February we celebrate
Two men who made our country great.
As presidents each led the way,
And we remember to this day
They worked for freedom and liberty,
They built America for you and me.

— Reproducible Page —

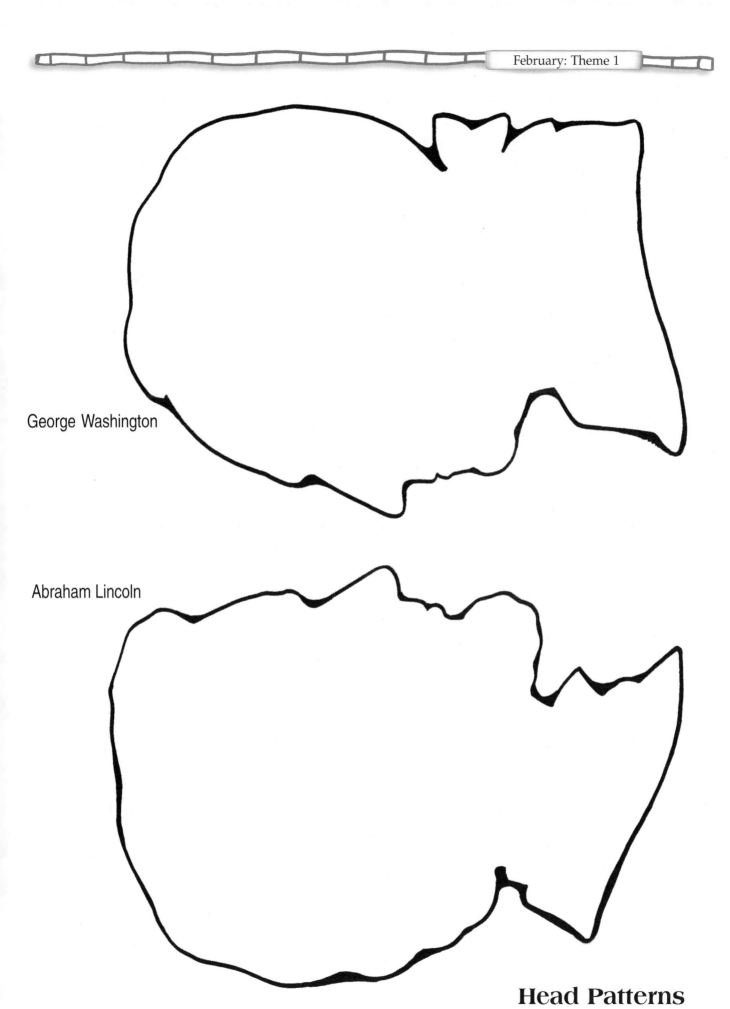

George Washington

Abraham Lincoln

# Head Patterns

# Literature LINK

- *Raining Valentines* by Felicia Bond
- *A Charlie Brown Valentine* by Justine Corman
- *Franklin's Valentines* by Paulette Bourgeois
- *The Valentine Bears* by Eve Bunting

## Be My Valentine

Love is lovely,
Love is divine—
Won't you be my
Valentine?
You're my good friend,
That I know,
Please, dear Valentine,
Don't say no.

## ACTIVITIES ➤

### SKILL CODES

## A, B, C, E, H, I, J

## Estimation Jar

- Fill a jar with candy conversation hearts. Ask each student to estimate how many hearts it took to fill the jar. Count the hearts and see who had the best estimate.

## Comparison and Weight

- Fill three different-size paper cups with conversation hearts.
- Ask students: "Which do you think is the heaviest? Why?"
- Weigh the cups and compare.

## Estimation and Comparison

- Talk with students about how to make a good estimate. To help students visualize different estimates, try using a number line or a 100's chart. For example, you might place 45 conversation hearts in a jar and then highlight a section of numbers on your 100's chart, let's say, 30 to 60. Then ask your students to estimate how many hearts are in the jar, pointing out that the actual number is in the highlighted section of the 100's chart between 30 and 60. This visual range helps students learn to estimate more accurately.

- Estimate how many hearts are in the small cup. Count them. Ask students: "Whose estimate is the closest?"

- Pour these hearts into a medium-size cup and estimate how many more hearts it will take to fill the cup. Count the hearts as you add them to the cup. Ask students: "Who made the best estimate?"

- Pour these hearts into a large-size cup and make an estimate as to how many more hearts it will take to fill this cup. Count the hearts as you add them to the large cup. Ask students: "Who made the best estimate?"

## Create the Calendar

# Directions

1. Reproduce each pattern onto the suggested paper (see "Calendar Components").

2. Provide each student with the calendar components, and with your class complete the following steps:

3. Cut out the pattern pieces.

4. Color in the phrase "I love you" across their pink heart cut-outs.

5. Glue the first stem vertically in the middle of the top half of the red construction paper (above the calendar); glue the second stem diagonally over the first, then glue the third stem diagonally over the second so they form an X (refer to the completed calendar illustration).

6. Glue a pink heart on the end of each stem (left to right, starting with the "I" heart).

7. Glue the "leaves" (the two green hearts) over where the stems cross.

8. Glue the poem in a bottom corner of the top half of the red construction paper (above the calendar).

9. Optional: Using glitter glue or markers, the students may decorate the hearts, being careful not to cover the lettering.

## Calendar Components

### Each student will need:

- 1 February Calendar affixed to the bottom half of a 12" x 18" piece of red construction paper

- 1 poem

- 2 small hearts (reproduce on green paper)

- 3 large hearts (reproduce on pink paper): The phrase "I love you" is written across the hearts for students to color or decorate. If you would prefer students to write independently, just Wite-Out the words before you reproduce the hearts.

- 3 stems (approximately $^3/_8$" x 7"; cut from green paper with a paper cutter)

## Be My Valentine

Love is lovely,
Love is divine—
Won't you be my Valentine?
You're my good friend,
That I know,
Please, dear Valentine,
Don't say no.

## Be My Valentine

Love is lovely,
Love is divine—
Won't you be my Valentine?
You're my good friend,
That I know,
Please, dear Valentine,
Don't say no.

## Be My Valentine

Love is lovely,
Love is divine—
Won't you be my Valentine?
You're my good friend,
That I know,
Please, dear Valentine,
Don't say no.

## Be My Valentine

Love is lovely,
Love is divine—
Won't you be my Valentine?
You're my good friend,
That I know,
Please, dear Valentine,
Don't say no.

## Be My Valentine

Love is lovely,
Love is divine—
Won't you be my Valentine?
You're my good friend,
That I know,
Please, dear Valentine,
Don't say no.

## Be My Valentine

Love is lovely,
Love is divine—
Won't you be my Valentine?
You're my good friend,
That I know,
Please, dear Valentine,
Don't say no.

— Reproducible Page —

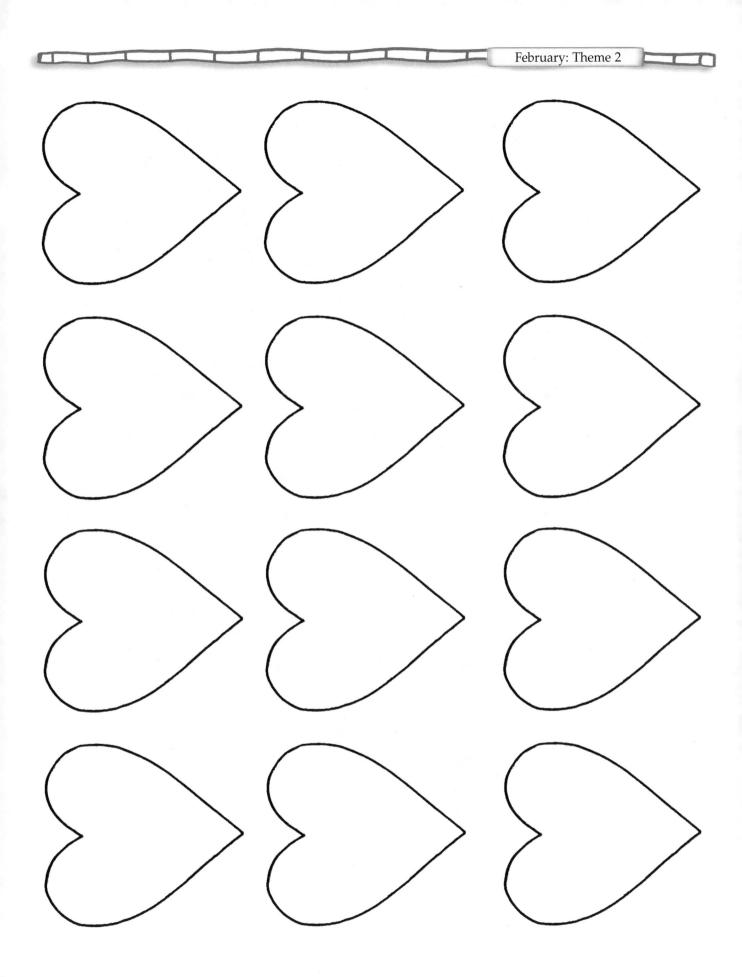

## Small Heart Pattern

# Heart Patterns

## Heart Patterns

# Fun Celebrations for February

## February 1

- Today is Freedom Day, marking the anniversary of President Abraham Lincoln's approval of the Thirteenth Amendment to the U.S. Constitution. This amendment abolished slavery.
- Today is also the first day of National African American History Month.
- Today also begins National Wild Bird Feeding month. To celebrate this occasion with your class, make wild bird feeders. Simply spread peanut butter on a pine cone or corn husk and roll it in birdseed. Hang these feeders on the trees that surround your school.

## February 2

It's Groundhog Day! Go outside and look for your shadow, just like our friend the groundhog will do. If you see your shadow, you can expect six weeks of chilly weather to follow. If you don't see your shadow, spring will arrive in six weeks.

## February 6

This date in 1996 marks the day the 100 billionth Crayola crayon was produced. Did you know that Crayola Crayons have been available since 1903 and that the word "Crayola" means oily chalk in French? Color a picture to celebrate the advent of these crafty crayons!

## February 7

Today is Laura Ingalls Wilder's birthday. Ingalls Wilder is the popular author of heartwarming stories about the American frontier. Drink some warm apple cider and enjoy a chapter from *Little House in the Big Woods*.

## February 12

Happy Birthday to Abraham Lincoln. The sixteenth president of the United States was born on this day in 1809.

## February 14

Today is Valentine's Day and National Have-a-Heart Day. Don't just pass out valentines to your students; discuss how to have a healthy heart by exercising daily and making good food choices.

## February 22

Happy Birthday to our first president. George Washington was born on this day in 1732.

## February 25

On this day in 1841 French impressionist painter Pierre-Auguste Renoir was born. Celebrate this artist by painting pictures in class today.

# March

## Theme 1:
## Kites

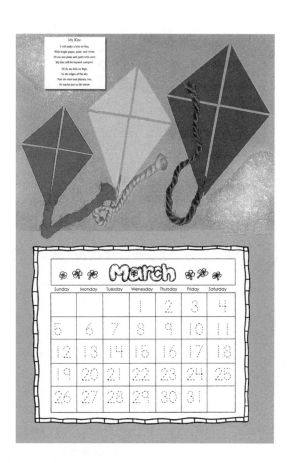

## Theme 2:
## St. Patrick's Day

# Literature LINK

- *The Legend of the Kite* by Chen Jiang Hong
- *Kite Flying* by Grace Lin
- *Kites: Magic Wishes That Fly up to the Sky* by Hitz Demi

## My Kite

I will make a kite so fine,
With bright paper, paint, and twine.
I'll cut and paste and paint with care;
My kite will be beyond compare.

I'll fly my kite so high,
To the edges of the sky,
Past the stars and planets, too,
Or maybe just to the moon.

## ACTIVITIES ➤

### SKILL CODES

## A, C, F, G, I, K

## Kite Sort

- Make several different colored kites using the pattern provided.
- Laminate each kite.
- Have your students sort the kites by color and count how many kites they have in each color group.

## Shape Kites

- Share a book that shows the many different varieties of kites.
- Give students different shapes cut from colored construction paper scraps. Encourage them to make their own creative kites and then share their kites with the class.

## Kite Tail Patterns

- Pre-make a variety of colored kite tails using construction paper, felt, or ribbon.

• Ask your students to create patterns using these kite tails. Begin with simple patterns and progress to more complex patterns. For example, for a simple pattern exercise, you might photocopy the bow pattern on different colors of paper; use without the tail. A more complex patterning activity might involve asking students to pattern with kite tails of varying colors, lengths, and materials.

## Create the Calendar

1. Reproduce each pattern onto the suggested paper (see "Calendar Components").

2. Provide each student with the calendar components, and with your class complete the following steps:

3. Cut out the pattern pieces.

4. Create clouds in the upper left- and lower right-hand corners of the top portion of the calendar page (above the actual calendar).

5. Place the poem within the cloud located in the top left-hand corner.

6. Piece together the kite puzzles (as shown in the illustration). Glue the kite tails to the bottom tip of each kite, allowing the tails to hang free. For added decoration, glue a bow to the surface where the kite and tail meet.

## Calendar Components

### Each student will need:

• 1 March Calendar affixed to the bottom half of a 12" x 18" piece of light-blue construction paper

• 1 poem

• 1 small kite (reproduce on red paper); 1 medium-size kite (reproduce on yellow paper); 1 large kite (reproduce on dark-blue paper)

• 1 five-inch yarn tail (red); 1 seven-inch yarn tail (yellow); 1 nine-inch yarn tail (dark blue)

• 3 bows (reproduce on various colored papers)

• material for making clouds: white crayon, cotton balls, polyester batting, etc.

## My Kite

I will make a kite so fine,
With bright paper, paint, and twine.
I'll cut and paste and paint with care;
My kite will be beyond compare.

I'll fly my kite so high,
To the edges of the sky,
Past the stars and planets, too,
Or maybe just to the moon.

## My Kite

I will make a kite so fine,
With bright paper, paint, and twine.
I'll cut and paste and paint with care;
My kite will be beyond compare.

I'll fly my kite so high,
To the edges of the sky,
Past the stars and planets, too,
Or maybe just to the moon.

## My Kite

I will make a kite so fine,
With bright paper, paint, and twine.
I'll cut and paste and paint with care;
My kite will be beyond compare.

I'll fly my kite so high,
To the edges of the sky,
Past the stars and planets, too,
Or maybe just to the moon.

## My Kite

I will make a kite so fine,
With bright paper, paint, and twine.
I'll cut and paste and paint with care;
My kite will be beyond compare.

I'll fly my kite so high,
To the edges of the sky,
Past the stars and planets, too,
Or maybe just to the moon.

## My Kite

I will make a kite so fine,
With bright paper, paint, and twine.
I'll cut and paste and paint with care;
My kite will be beyond compare.

I'll fly my kite so high,
To the edges of the sky,
Past the stars and planets, too,
Or maybe just to the moon.

## My Kite

I will make a kite so fine,
With bright paper, paint, and twine.
I'll cut and paste and paint with care;
My kite will be beyond compare.

I'll fly my kite so high,
To the edges of the sky,
Past the stars and planets, too,
Or maybe just to the moon.

— Reproducible Page —

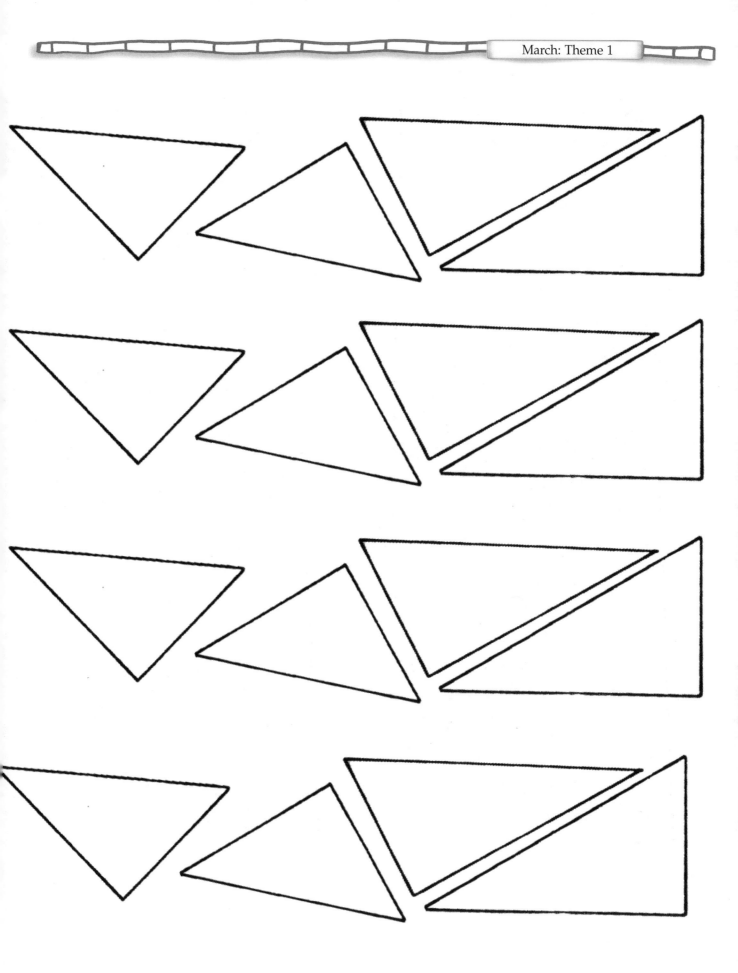

# Small Kite Pattern

# Medium Kite Pattern

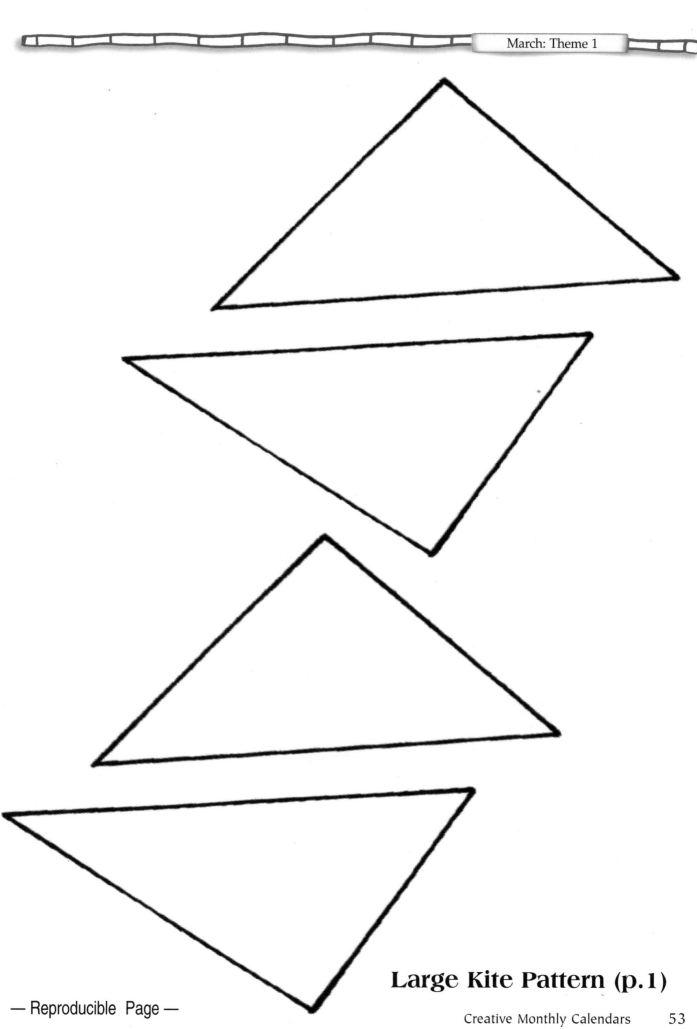

**Large Kite Pattern (p.1)**

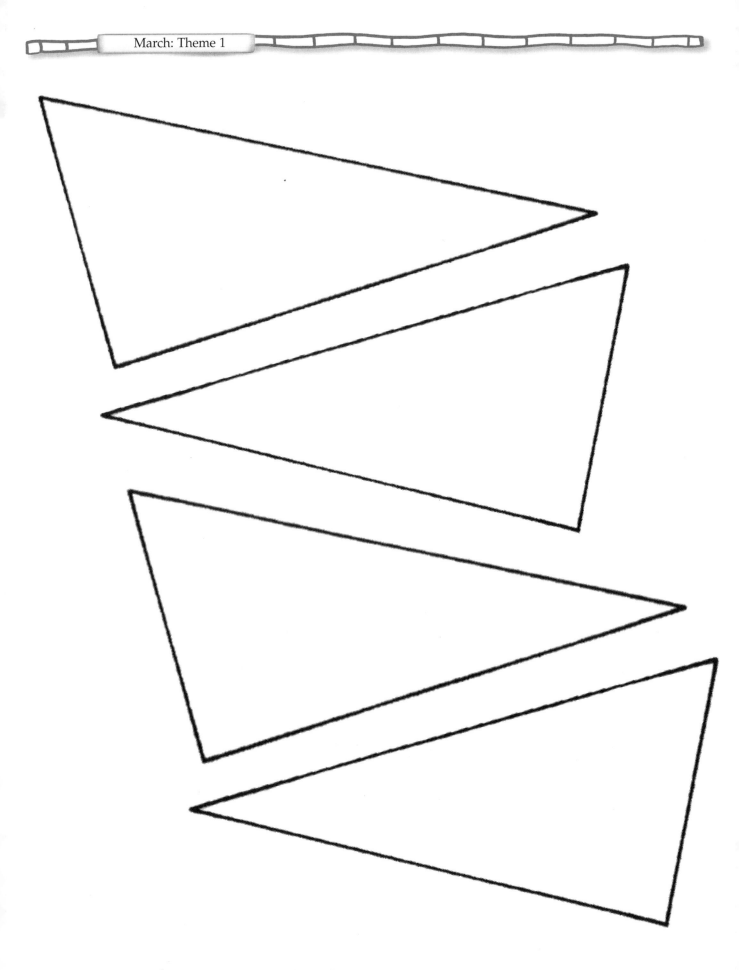

March: Theme 1

# Large Kite Pattern (p.2)

— Reproducible Page —

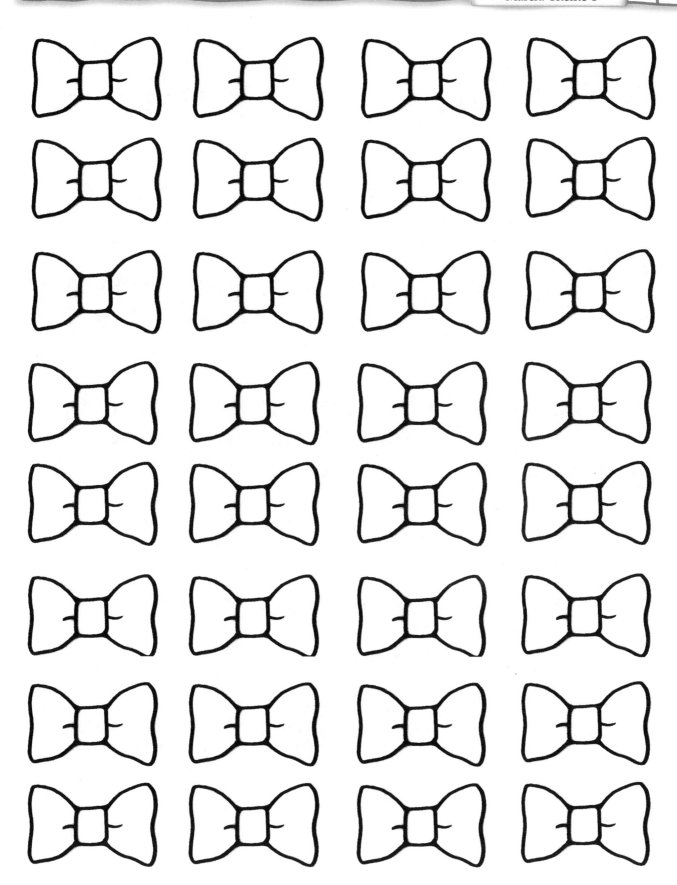

# Bow Pattern for Kite

— Reproducible Page —

# Literature LINK

- *St. Patrick's Day* by Gail Gibbons
- *Leprechaun's Gold* by Teresa Bateman
- *St. Patrick's Day in the Morning* by Eve Bunting

## Lucky Leprechaun

Lucky little leprechaun,
Oh, everybody knows,
At the end of each rainbow
You keep a pot of gold.

Lucky little leprechaun,
I'll travel here and there.
Maybe soon I'll catch you,
And then you'll have to share.

## ACTIVITIES ➤

## SKILL CODES

## A, B, C, D, I

## Pot-o-Gold Addition/Subtraction

- Use plastic or chocolate foil-covered gold coins to create addition or subtraction sentences. For example, you might say to students:

"In the leprechaun's pot there are five (5) gold coins. If I take two (2) out, then there will be three (3) coins left in the pot." (5 - 2 = 3)

"If a leprechaun found four (4) pieces of gold and added them to the two (2) he already had in his pot, how many pieces of gold does he have altogether?" (4 + 2 = 6)

## Coin Sort

- Use real coins for a sorting activity. Sort the pennies into one pot, the nickels into a second pot, and the dimes into a third. How many coins are in each pot? How much money does that equal in each pot? How much money altogether?

## Coin Count

- Use real money to make addition or subtraction sentences. You might say to students:

"In my pot there is one (1) dime ($.10) and one (1) nickel ($.5). I have fifteen cents ($.15) total." ($.10 + $.5 = $.15)

## Create the Calendar

# Directions

1. Reproduce each pattern onto the suggested paper (see "Calendar Components").

2. Trace and/or cut out the pattern pieces. Trace the pot pattern onto cardboard and cut to create one or more templates for the pot of gold.

3. Provide each student with the calendar components, and with your class complete the following steps:

4. Using the pre-made template, trace the pot on black construction paper. Cut out the pattern. Glue the pot to the top portion of the calendar page (just above the calendar).

5. Glue the gold above the pot, making sure to overlap some of the individual pieces.

6. Glue the leprechaun face just above the pot of gold.

7. Glue the orange yarn pieces to the back side of the leprechaun hat.

8. Turn the hat over and glue it to the leprechaun face. As shown in the calendar illustration, the hat will extend above the calendar page. Keep this in mind when you're applying glue to the hat.

9. Ask students to trace their hands on tan- or peach-colored construction paper. Cut out the hand patterns and glue to either side of the pot. Or, reproduce the hand patterns on tan paper and provide each student with one set.

10. Paint three green shamrocks on either side of the pot of gold as follows:

    - Paint three short stems on each side with a small brush or cotton swab; add three or four leaves by dipping a finger into the paint and touching it on the paper at the top of each stem.

11. Optional: Add sparkle to each calendar by outlining the shamrocks and hat with gold glitter.

## Calendar Components

### Each student will need:

- 1 March Calendar affixed to the bottom half of a 12" x 18" piece of light-blue construction paper

- 1 poem

- 1 leprechaun face (reproduce on tan or peach paper)

- tan or peach paper (for students to use to trace their hands)

- 1 pot (trace on black construction paper)

- 1 hat (reproduce on green paper)

- gold coins (reproduce on gold paper)

- orange yarn for strands of leprechaun hair

## Lucky Leprechaun

Lucky little leprechaun,
Oh, everybody knows,
At the end of each rainbow
You keep a pot of gold.

Lucky little leprechaun,
I'll travel here and there.
Maybe soon I'll catch you,
And then you'll have to share.

## Lucky Leprechaun

Lucky little leprechaun,
Oh, everybody knows,
At the end of each rainbow
You keep a pot of gold.

Lucky little leprechaun,
I'll travel here and there.
Maybe soon I'll catch you,
And then you'll have to share.

## Lucky Leprechaun

Lucky little leprechaun,
Oh, everybody knows,
At the end of each rainbow
You keep a pot of gold.

Lucky little leprechaun,
I'll travel here and there.
Maybe soon I'll catch you,
And then you'll have to share.

## Lucky Leprechaun

Lucky little leprechaun,
Oh, everybody knows,
At the end of each rainbow
You keep a pot of gold.

Lucky little leprechaun,
I'll travel here and there.
Maybe soon I'll catch you,
And then you'll have to share.

## Lucky Leprechaun

Lucky little leprechaun,
Oh, everybody knows,
At the end of each rainbow
You keep a pot of gold.

Lucky little leprechaun,
I'll travel here and there.
Maybe soon I'll catch you,
And then you'll have to share.

## Lucky Leprechaun

Lucky little leprechaun,
Oh, everybody knows,
At the end of each rainbow
You keep a pot of gold.

Lucky little leprechaun,
I'll travel here and there.
Maybe soon I'll catch you,
And then you'll have to share.

**Leprechaun Pattern**

# Pot Pattern

— Reproducible Page —

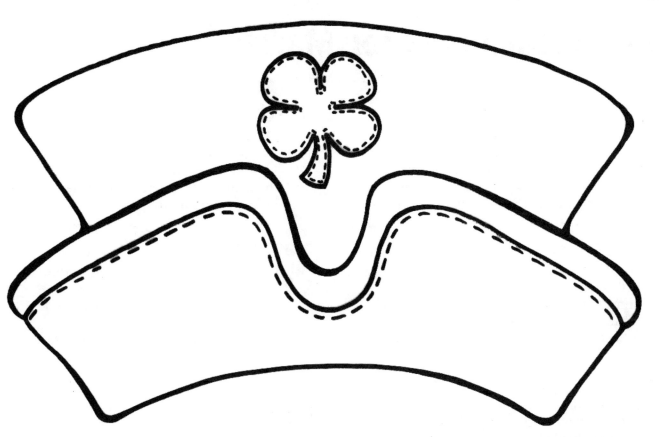

**Hat Pattern**

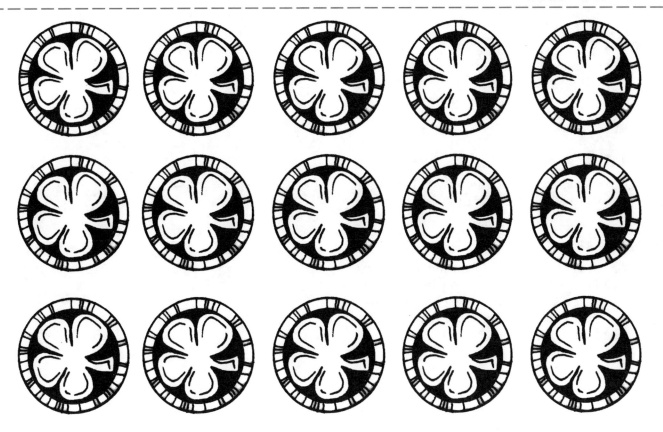

**Coin Pattern**

# Fun Celebrations for March

## March 2

Theodore Seuss Geisel, better known as Dr. Seuss, was born on this day in 1904. Enjoy some green eggs and ham with your class, and read some Dr. Seuss classics together. Create some fun Dr. Seuss rhymes of your own.

## March 3

On this day in 1931 "The Star Spangled Banner" became our national anthem. Sing the anthem loud and strong as a salute to our country.

## March 7

This is the day the popular board game Monopoly was invented by Charles Darrow. Celebrate this 1933 anniversary by playing some of your favorite board games.

## March 8

Honor International Working Women's Day by inviting your students' moms to visit the class to share information about their careers.

## March 9

If you feel stressed out today, you have a good excuse—today is National Panic Day!

## March 10

Alexander Graham Bell transmitted the first telephone message on this day in 1876. This is a perfect day to practice telephone manners, learn about 911, or make paper-cup telephones.

## March 12

The United States Post Office was established on this day in 1789. Take a trip to your local post office to learn about how the mail system operates. Write and mail a letter to your family.

## March 17

Celebrate St. Patrick's Day by reading Irish folk tales about leprechauns and their pots of gold. Hide chocolate gold coins in your classroom and let your students search for them. This is also a great day to learn about rainbows and how they are formed.

## March 26

Today is "Make up Your Own Holiday" day. This is a wonderful chance for your students to let their imaginations soar when creating their own special holiday.

# April

## Theme 1: Baby Rabbits

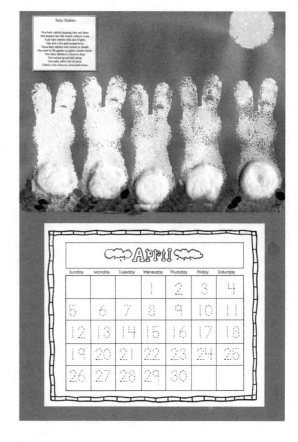

## Theme 2: April Showers

# Literature LINK

- *Bunny Cakes* by Rosemary Wells
- *The Velveteen Rabbit* by Margery Williams Bianco
- *Good Night Moon* by Margaret Wise Brown
- *Guess How Much I Love You* by Sam McBratney

## Baby Rabbits *

Five baby rabbits hopping here and there,
One hopped into the woods without a care.
Four baby rabbits with ears of gray,
One saw a fox and hopped away.
Three baby rabbits with carrots to munch,
One went to the garden to gather another bunch.
Two baby rabbits in a burrow deep,
One curled up and fell asleep.
One baby rabbit left all alone,
Called to the others to come back home.

## ACTIVITIES ➤

### SKILL CODES

## A, B, C, D, I

## Size Comparison

- Reproduce the rabbit patterns on gray construction paper. Laminate.
- Photocopy the word and symbol cards: larger (>), smaller (<), and same (=). Cut apart and laminate each card.
- Direct students to situate two rabbits side by side. Place the correct card underneath each to indicate size comparison.

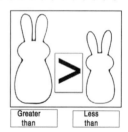
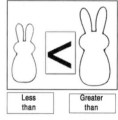
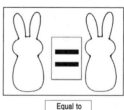

## Amount Comparison

- Using the reproduced rabbit patterns or plastic rabbit counters, have the students make two sets of rabbits (e.g., one set of three rabbits and another set of four; and two even sets).
- Count the rabbits in each set and then place the correct symbol in between the sets to indicate if the first set is greater than, less than, or equal to the second set.

*Finger-Play

# Subtraction

- Make five stick puppets using the rabbit patterns.
- Provide five students with one stick puppet each. Using the stick puppets as props, have these students act out the poem "Baby Rabbits."
- Ask students to make subtraction stories of their own. For example:

  "There were five (5) rabbits playing in the field. Two (2) became tired and went home to take a nap. How many rabbits were left playing in the field?" (5 - 2 = 3)

## Create the Calendar

# Directions

1. Use the smallest rabbit pattern to create a sponge print. Simply cut out the pattern, place it on the compressed sponge, trace around the edges, and then cut the rabbit out. Compressed sponge works the best, but a regular sponge also works well.

2. Cut a circle (2" dia.) from the sponge for the sun.

3. Provide each student with the calendar components, and with your class complete the following steps:

4. Daub sponge scraps in green paint to create a grass border along the top portion of the calendar page.

5. Using the circle sponge, print a yellow sun in the upper right-hand corner of the calendar page. Allow the grass and sun to dry. For a brighter yellow, use a circle sponge to print a white sun first. Allow to dry, then with another circle sponge, print over the white circle with yellow.

6. Glue the poem in the upper left-hand corner of the calendar page.

7. Sponge-paint rabbits across the bottom of the picture (overlap the grass slightly). Rabbits can be any color.

8. Add fluffy tails to each rabbit.

9. Optional: Have students dip the tips of their fingers into different colored pastel fingerpaints to print eggs in the grass.

## Calendar Components

### Each student will need:

- 1 April Calendar affixed to the bottom half of a 12" x 18" piece of light-blue construction paper
- 1 poem
- access to sponges crafted in the following shapes: baby rabbit (use the smallest rabbit pattern), 2" circle (sun), grass (use sponge scraps to print grass)
- access to paints in a variety of colors (green, yellow, pastels)
- cotton balls or polyester batting for bunny tails

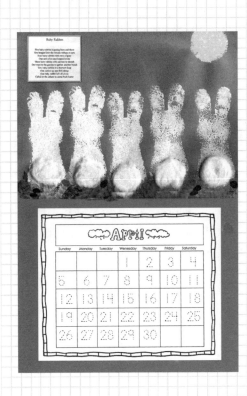

## Baby Rabbits
Five baby rabbits hopping here and there,
One hopped into the woods without a care.
Four baby rabbits with ears of gray,
One saw a fox and hopped away.
Three baby rabbits with carrots to munch,
One went to the garden to gather another bunch.
Two baby rabbits in a burrow deep,
One curled up and fell asleep.
One baby rabbit left all alone,
Called to the others to come back home.

## Baby Rabbits
Five baby rabbits hopping here and there,
One hopped into the woods without a care.
Four baby rabbits with ears of gray,
One saw a fox and hopped away.
Three baby rabbits with carrots to munch,
One went to the garden to gather another bunch.
Two baby rabbits in a burrow deep,
One curled up and fell asleep.
One baby rabbit left all alone,
Called to the others to come back home.

## Baby Rabbits
Five baby rabbits hopping here and there,
One hopped into the woods without a care.
Four baby rabbits with ears of gray,
One saw a fox and hopped away.
Three baby rabbits with carrots to munch,
One went to the garden to gather another bunch.
Two baby rabbits in a burrow deep,
One curled up and fell asleep.
One baby rabbit left all alone,
Called to the others to come back home.

## Baby Rabbits
Five baby rabbits hopping here and there,
One hopped into the woods without a care.
Four baby rabbits with ears of gray,
One saw a fox and hopped away.
Three baby rabbits with carrots to munch,
One went to the garden to gather another bunch.
Two baby rabbits in a burrow deep,
One curled up and fell asleep.
One baby rabbit left all alone,
Called to the others to come back home.

## Baby Rabbits
Five baby rabbits hopping here and there,
One hopped into the woods without a care.
Four baby rabbits with ears of gray,
One saw a fox and hopped away.
Three baby rabbits with carrots to munch,
One went to the garden to gather another bunch.
Two baby rabbits in a burrow deep,
One curled up and fell asleep.
One baby rabbit left all alone,
Called to the others to come back home.

## Baby Rabbits
Five baby rabbits hopping here and there,
One hopped into the woods without a care.
Four baby rabbits with ears of gray,
One saw a fox and hopped away.
Three baby rabbits with carrots to munch,
One went to the garden to gather another bunch.
Two baby rabbits in a burrow deep,
One curled up and fell asleep.
One baby rabbit left all alone,
Called to the others to come back home.

— Reproducible Page —

## Rabbit Patterns

|  | Less than |
| --- | --- |
|  | Greater than |
|  | Equal to |

— Reproducible Page —

## Small Rabbit Pattern

# Literature LINK

- *Come On, Rain!* by Karen Hesse
- *Down Comes the Rain* by Franklin Mansfield Branley
- *Rain Song* by Lezlie Evans
- *Rain! Rain!* by Carol Greene

### Rain

2 - 4 - 6 - 8: Rain is coming,
I can't wait.

5 - 10 - 15 - 20: When it comes,
I hope there's plenty.

10 - 20 - 30 - 40: I know the rain
Will be here shortly.

25 - 50 - 75 - 100: I love the rain,
But not the thunder!

## ACTIVITIES ➤

## SKILL CODES

## A, C, I

## Odd and Even

- Reduce and reproduce 10 ducks on 1 piece of colored paper and 10 ducks on another piece of colored paper.
- Write the numbers 1 through 20 on the ducks. Place all the odd numbers on one color and all the even numbers on the other color.
- Cut the ducks out and laminate them to make flashcards.
- Have your students build a number line. Ask students: "Which color represents the odd numbers? Let's skip-count by two, counting all the odd numbers. Which color represents the even numbers? Let's skip-count by two, counting all the even numbers."

## Skip-Counting

- Use the same duck flashcards from the above activity to make another number line. This time have the students place a square piece of construction paper underneath all the numbers that you can count to by five. This square piece of construction paper should be a different color than the flashcards and large enough to frame the flashcards.
- Count the numbers by fives. Repeat for numbers that can be counted to by tens, but this time use a slightly larger piece of different colored paper, one large enough to frame the previous frame and flashcard. Count the numbers by 10. Ask students: "Are the numbers that can be counted to by fives

odd, even, or some of both? Are the numbers that can be counted to by tens odd, even, or some of both?"

# Flashcard Fun

- Use the same flashcards as above.
- Hold one flashcard up in front of the group and ask them to tell you whether the number is odd or even. See who can guess the answer the quickest. This can become a game by asking two students to stand up at one time. The student who guesses the answer the fastest gets to try again with the next student. Whoever answers the question the fastest remains standing. The winner is the person who answers the most correctly in succession.

## Create the Calendar

# Directions

1. Reproduce each pattern onto the suggested paper (see "Calendar Components").

2. Provide each student with the calendar components, and with your class complete the following steps:

3. Cut out the pattern pieces. Be sure when the students cut out the ducks, you cut around the wing so students will be able to slip the umbrella handles beneath.

4. Glue the poem to the lower right-hand corner of the calendar page (above the actual calander).

5. For each duck, color the beak orange. Color the boots red. Optional: glue on a wiggle-eye.

6. Decorate the umbrellas and slip underneath the wing. Glue the duck/umbrella to the calendar page.

7. Position raindrops back to back. Have students sandwich twine in between the raindrops; glue.

8. Position raindrops evenly across the calendar page, with the twine end at the top. Tape in place along the top edge of the calendar.

9. Glue clouds over the taped ends of the twine, allowing the actual raindrops to swing freely.

## Calendar Components

### Each student will need:

- 1 April Calendar affixed to the bottom half of a 12" x 18" piece of dark-blue construction paper
- 1 poem
- 1 duck (reproduce on yellow paper)
- 12 raindrops (reproduce on blue construction paper)
- 1 umbrella (reproduce on violet, green, or pink construction paper)
- 6 strands of twine or thin white yarn (varying lengths: 4"-6")
- cotton balls or polyester batting for clouds

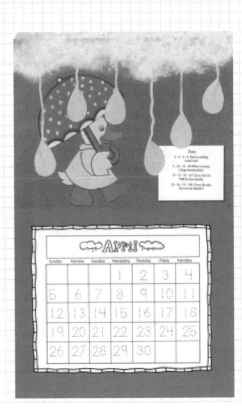

## Rain

2 - 4 - 6 - 8: Rain is coming,
I can't wait.

5 - 10 - 15 - 20: When it comes,
I hope there's plenty.

10 - 20 - 30 - 40: I know the rain
Will be here shortly.

25 - 50 - 75 - 100: I love the rain,
But not the thunder!

## Rain

2 - 4 - 6 - 8: Rain is coming,
I can't wait.

5 - 10 - 15 - 20: When it comes,
I hope there's plenty.

10 - 20 - 30 - 40: I know the rain
Will be here shortly.

25 - 50 - 75 - 100: I love the rain,
But not the thunder!

## Rain

2 - 4 - 6 - 8: Rain is coming,
I can't wait.

5 - 10 - 15 - 20: When it comes,
I hope there's plenty.

10 - 20 - 30 - 40: I know the rain
Will be here shortly.

25 - 50 - 75 - 100: I love the rain,
But not the thunder!

## Rain

2 - 4 - 6 - 8: Rain is coming,
I can't wait.

5 - 10 - 15 - 20: When it comes,
I hope there's plenty.

10 - 20 - 30 - 40: I know the rain
Will be here shortly.

25 - 50 - 75 - 100: I love the rain,
But not the thunder!

## Rain

2 - 4 - 6 - 8: Rain is coming,
I can't wait.

5 - 10 - 15 - 20: When it comes,
I hope there's plenty.

10 - 20 - 30 - 40: I know the rain
Will be here shortly.

25 - 50 - 75 - 100: I love the rain,
But not the thunder!

## Rain

2 - 4 - 6 - 8: Rain is coming,
I can't wait.

5 - 10 - 15 - 20: When it comes,
I hope there's plenty.

10 - 20 - 30 - 40: I know the rain
Will be here shortly.

25 - 50 - 75 - 100: I love the rain,
But not the thunder!

# Duck Pattern

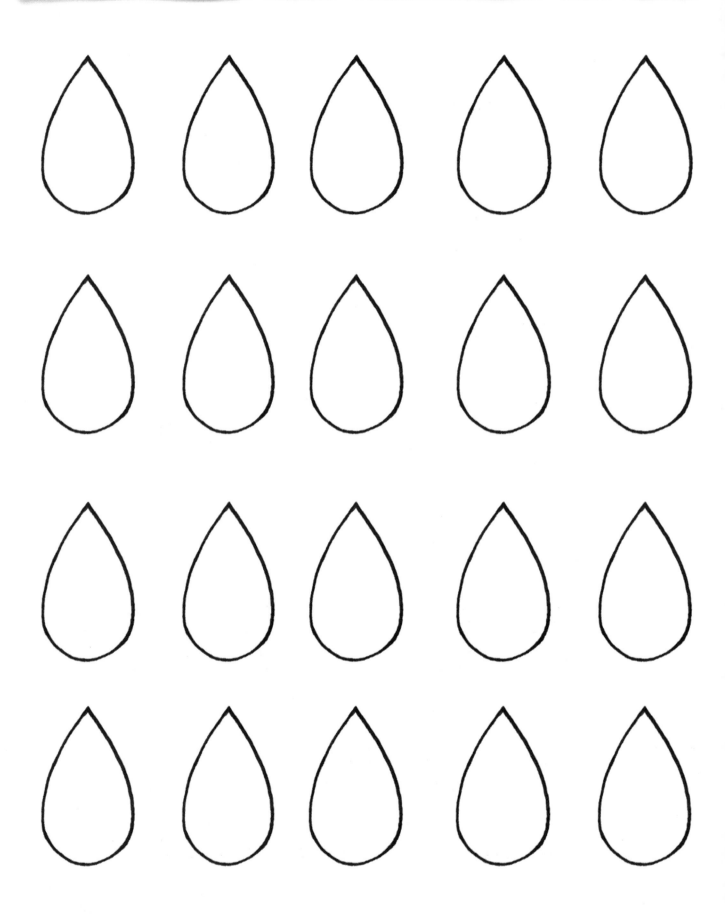

# Raindrop Pattern

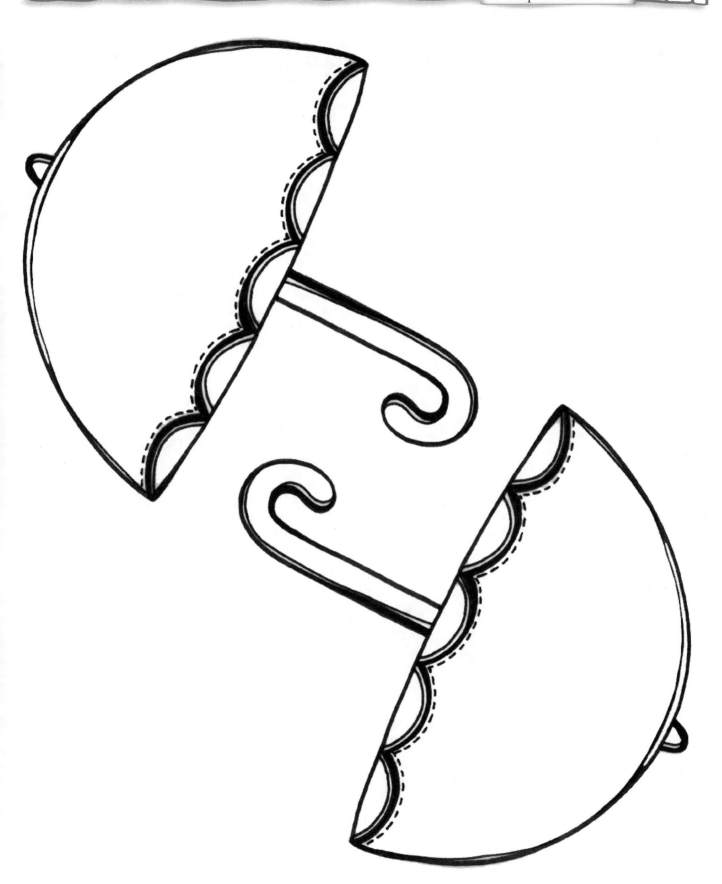

## Umbrella Pattern

# Fun Celebrations for April

## April 1

- Is today National No Homework Day? No, just fooling, it's April Fools' Day! Today is the day to have a few tricks up your sleeve!

- Today also marks the beginning of National Poetry Month. This is a great time to share some of your favorite poems with your class. Encourage students to write poems of their own.

## April 2

This is International Children's Book Day. Ask each student to bring in her/his favorite book to share with the class.

## April 7

Today is World Health Day. Discuss the importance of daily exercise with your students, and teach them an exercise, focusing on each major muscle group.

## April 9

Today is National School Librarian Day. Let your librarian know how much you appreciate her/him. You might even consider having your students read the librarian a book today.

## April 14

It's Moment of Laughter Day! Read a silly story or share a few riddles and jokes with your class to mark this hilarious occasion.

## April 15

The very first McDonald's opened today in 1955. Visit your local McDonald's and celebrate with a Happy Meal!

## April 21

Today is Kindergarten Day. This is a day to recognize the importance of play, games, and creativity in education. Have your students do buddy activities with the kindergarten kids today—read books to them, play games with them, or write them letters!

## April 22

Today is Earth Day. Discuss the importance of recycling, conservation, and maintaining our beautiful planet. To commemorate this day you might choose to plant a tree on your campus, create a classroom garden, or pick up trash on the playground.

# May

## Theme 1:
## Mother's Day

## Theme 2:
## Flowers

# Literature LINK

- *My Monster Mama Loves Me So* by Laura Leuck
- *What Mommies Do Best* by Laura Numeroff
- *The Mommy Book* by Todd Parr
- *Even Firefighters Hug Their Moms* by Christine Kole MacLean

## Mothers

Birds have mothers,
Mice have mothers,
Turtles have mothers too.
I'm the happiest child around
Because my mother is you!

## ACTIVITIES ➤

### SKILL CODES

## A, C, F, G, I, K

## Shape Mom

- Place a variety of shapes in a tub, including, but not limited to: paper cones, toilet paper rolls (cylinders), Styrofoam spheres, buttons, rectangles, circles, squares, diamonds, plastic jewels, yarn, construction paper shapes cut to form different size triangles.
- Have students create "Shape Moms" using material from the tub. If you decide to use hot or tacky glue, be sure to provide adult supervision.

## Shape Picnic

- Make a trip to your local grocery store to pick up edible items in a variety of shapes. Such items might include: ice cream cones, Hostess Ho-Ho cylinders, tangerine spheres, cookies, crackers and cereals of various shapes, lunch meat or cheese slices cut into shapes. Be as creative as you like!
- Once you have chosen your menu, invite students' mothers to attend a "Shape Snack and Tea." Serve your shape snack creations and iced tea to students' moms. Optional: Have students create special placemats for the occasion. Woven patterns and shape patterns are colorful and interesting.

## Calendar Components

### Each student will need:
- 1 May Calendar affixed to the bottom half of a 12" x 18" piece of lavender construction paper
- 1 poem
- 1 piece of white construction paper (4" x 5")
- 1 frame (color of each student's choosing) (6" x 7")
- material for decorating paper frame (buttons, beads, ribbon, etc.)

## Create the Calendar

# Directions

1. Glue the poem on the lower right corner of the calendar page (above the actual calendar).

2. Glue the pink paper to the left of it.

3. Have students draw a portrait of their mother on the white paper (or use the face pattern provided). Depending on the experience and ability of the students, it may be necessary to first model the details they should include: correct hair and eye color, eyebrows, eyelashes, etc.

4. Glue the completed portrait on the pink paper (or whichever color each student has chosen).

5. Decorate the picture frame with provided materials. Younger students will do better with fewer choices, while older students will enjoy the variety.

## Mothers

Birds have mothers,

Mice have mothers,

Turtles have mothers too.

I'm the happiest child around

Because my mother is you!

## Mothers

Birds have mothers,

Mice have mothers,

Turtles have mothers too.

I'm the happiest child around

Because my mother is you!

## Mothers

Birds have mothers,

Mice have mothers,

Turtles have mothers too.

I'm the happiest child around

Because my mother is you!

## Mothers

Birds have mothers,

Mice have mothers,

Turtles have mothers too.

I'm the happiest child around

Because my mother is you!

## Mothers

Birds have mothers,

Mice have mothers,

Turtles have mothers too.

I'm the happiest child around

Because my mother is you!

## Mothers

Birds have mothers,

Mice have mothers,

Turtles have mothers too.

I'm the happiest child around

Because my mother is you!

— Reproducible Page —

# Face Pattern

# Frame Pattern

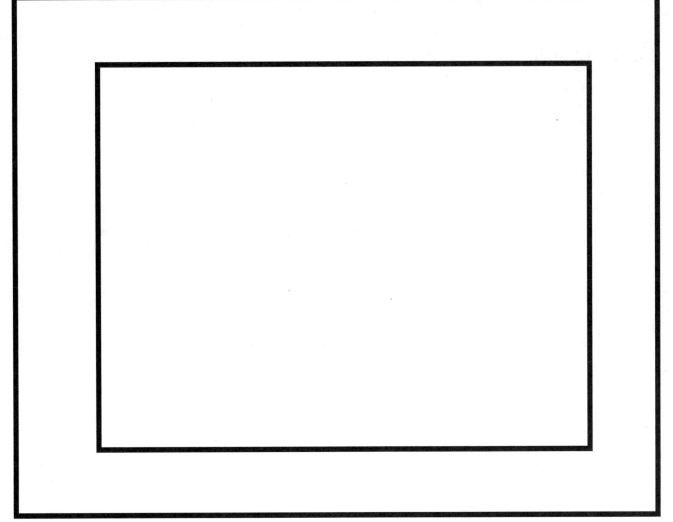

# Literature LINK

- *Alison's Zinnia* by Anita Lobel
- *Sunflower House* by Eve Bunting
- *Planting a Rainbow* by Lois Ehlert
- *From Seed to Plant* by Gail Gibbons

## Flowers

In my garden
There's a rainbow
Of flowers, fragrant and bright.
Cheerful blossoms bloom and glow;
They're such a beautiful sight.

Purple, red and gentle pink,
Yellow, white, and blue—
Enjoying a flower garden
Is a wonderful thing to do.

# ACTIVITIES ➤

## SKILL CODES

### A, B, C, I, K

## Flower Sort

- Bring in a variety of fresh or dried flowers.
- Ask students to sort and classify the flowers.
- What was the sorting rule each child used? Did they sort by color, shape, or size?
- Optional: Do the same activity using the pinwheel flower pattern (photocopy in various colors and sizes).

## Flower Pattern

- Using a die-cut machine, cut flowers in many different colors. If your school or district does not own a die-cut machine, you can look for pre-cut flowers at craft stores, scrapbook stores, or teacher-supply stores.
- Give students a long piece of green yarn.
- Have them lay a flower pattern on the yarn.
- Once the pattern has been checked for accuracy, have each student affix the flowers to the yarn using glue or a stapler. The finished product will be a vine (or garland) of patterned flowers.

## Calendar Components

### Each student will need:

- 1 May Calendar affixed to the bottom half of a 12" x 18" piece of light-blue construction paper

- 1 poem

- 3-5 pinwheel flowers, various sizes and colors (reproduce on paper, various colors)

- 1-2 green leaves (reproduce on green paper)

- 1 stem/flower, approximately $^3/_8$" x 6" (reproduce on green paper)

- 1 basket (reproduce on yellow paper)

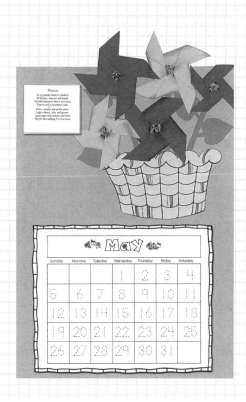

## Create the Calendar

# Directions

1. Reproduce each pattern onto the suggested paper (see "Calendar Components").

2. Provide each student with the calendar components, and with your class complete the following steps:

3. Cut out the pattern pieces.

4. Fold the flowers as shown, staple in center, and glue on the stems.

5. Position the basket and flowers on the page (above the actual calendar grid). Slide the basket to one side to provide room to glue the poem in place. When properly spaced, glue each piece to the surface of the paper.

6. Glue birdseed or glitter to the center of each flower. Glue the completed flowers in the basket. Flowers may extend beyond the edge of the paper.

### Flowers

In my garden
There's a rainbow
Of flowers, fragrant and bright.
Cheerful blossoms bloom and glow;
They're such a beautiful sight.

Purple, red and gentle pink,
Yellow, white, and blue—
Enjoying a flower garden
Is a wonderful thing to do.

### Flowers

In my garden
There's a rainbow
Of flowers, fragrant and bright.
Cheerful blossoms bloom and glow;
They're such a beautiful sight.

Purple, red and gentle pink,
Yellow, white, and blue—
Enjoying a flower garden
Is a wonderful thing to do.

### Flowers

In my garden
There's a rainbow
Of flowers, fragrant and bright.
Cheerful blossoms bloom and glow;
They're such a beautiful sight.

Purple, red and gentle pink,
Yellow, white, and blue—
Enjoying a flower garden
Is a wonderful thing to do.

### Flowers

In my garden
There's a rainbow
Of flowers, fragrant and bright.
Cheerful blossoms bloom and glow;
They're such a beautiful sight.

Purple, red and gentle pink,
Yellow, white, and blue—
Enjoying a flower garden
Is a wonderful thing to do.

### Flowers

In my garden
There's a rainbow
Of flowers, fragrant and bright.
Cheerful blossoms bloom and glow;
They're such a beautiful sight.

Purple, red and gentle pink,
Yellow, white, and blue—
Enjoying a flower garden
Is a wonderful thing to do.

### Flowers

In my garden
There's a rainbow
Of flowers, fragrant and bright.
Cheerful blossoms bloom and glow;
They're such a beautiful sight.

Purple, red and gentle pink,
Yellow, white, and blue—
Enjoying a flower garden
Is a wonderful thing to do.

— Reproducible Page —

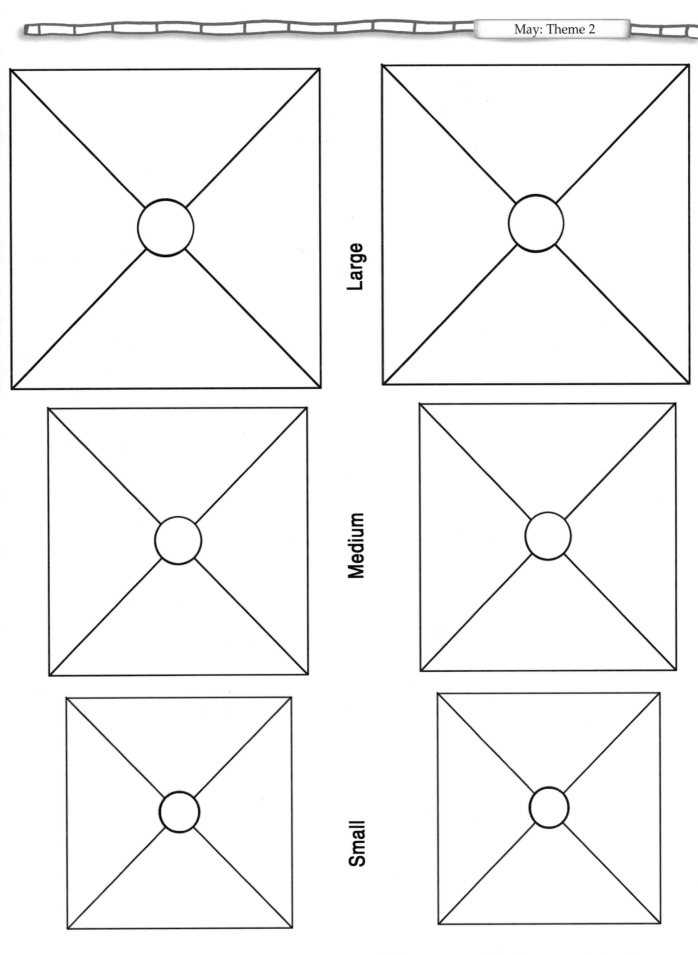

Large

Medium

Small

# Pinwheel Flower Patterns

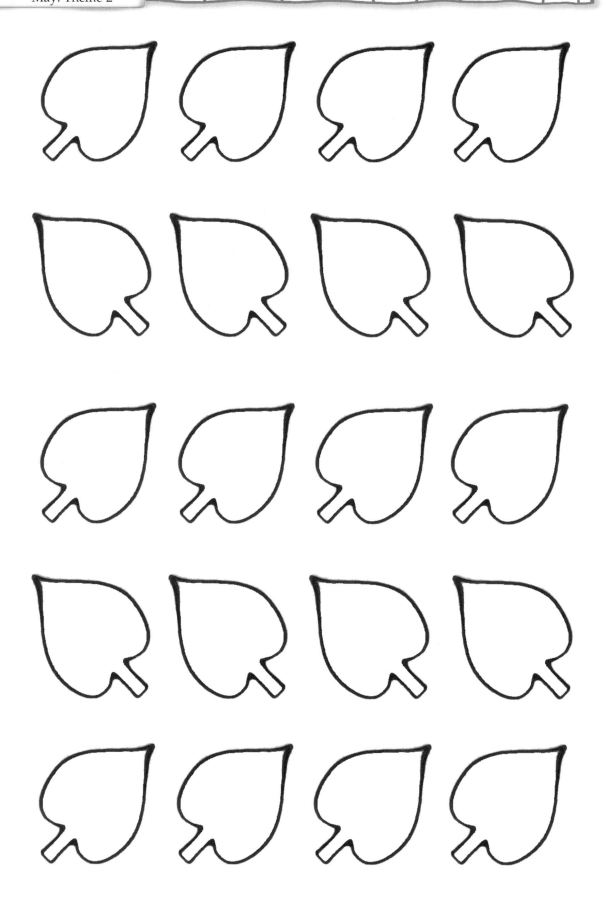

# Flower Leaf Pattern

— Reproducible  Page —

**Flower Basket Pattern**

# Fun Celebrations for May

## May 1

Today is Mother Goose Day. Ask your students to share their favorite Mother Goose rhyme with the class.

## May 4

- Today is National Day of the Teacher. This is a day to honor those who encourage, inspire, and teach our children. That just happens to be you, so be sure to do something nice for yourself today!

- This is also National Weather Observers' Day. Keep a chart or graph of the weather with your students this week.

## May 5

May 5 is Cinco de Mayo. Mexicans everywhere celebrate General Ignacio Zaragoza's victory over the invading French forces in 1862. Children love to hit a candy-filled piñata, so consider having a piñata party with your class today.

## May 7

Today is Pyotr Ilich Tchaikovsky's birthday. Plan a field trip to see the ballet *The Sleeping Beauty* or *The Nutcracker* in his honor.

## May 8

Today is No Socks Day, so wear sandals and let those toes show!

## May 11

Today is Eat What You Want Day. Live it up and have a munch-and-crunch celebration in your class. Allow students to bring snacks to school to eat throughout the day.

## May 12

It's Limerick Day! Read a silly limerick or two and encourage your students to write their own limericks.

## May 18

Today is National Museum Day. This is a wonderful day to plan a field trip to one of your local museums.

## May 22

Arnold Lobel, author of the *Frog and Toad* series, was born on this day in 1933. Honor his birthday by reading one of the *Frog and Toad* stories to your class.

## May 23

Authors Margaret Wise Brown (*Goodnight Moon*) and Scott O'Dell (*Island of the Blue Dolphins*) were born on this day.

# June

## Theme 1:
## Father's Day

## Theme 2:
## School Is Out

# Literature LINK

- *Owl Moon* by Jane Yolen
- *What Daddies Do Best* by Laura Numeroff
- *The Daddy Book* by Todd Parr
- *I Love My Daddy Because* by Laurel Porter Gaylord

## My Dad

How do I measure my love for you—
In inches, or yards, or miles?
I could measure with rulers or
yardsticks too,
But I'd rather use hugs and smiles.

## ACTIVITIES ➤

### SKILL CODES

### A, C, H, I

## Standard and Non-Standard Measurement

- Use standard forms of measurement (e.g., inches, centimeters, pounds) or non-standard forms of measurement (e.g., Unifix cubes, blocks) to promote the understanding that objects have properties such as length, weight, and capacity.
- Have students measure and record the length of various classroom objects and record their results in a "measurement journal."
- Bring students together to share their findings.
- Using a scale, have students weigh common classroom objects. Ask students, for example: "How many Unifix cubes does a pencil weigh? How many grams does an eraser weigh?"

## Measurement of Time

- Make measurements of time such as second, minute, hour, day, month, and year.
- Write a daily schedule on the board using time. For example, you might discuss with students: "At 8:00 AM we open our class. At 8:30 AM we begin spelling. At 9:00 AM we begin reading groups."

• On the calendar mark special dates (such as Father's Day) and keep a counting graph measuring how many days until these dates arrive.

Discuss concepts such as how many months are left until the end of school; how many weeks your students have been in school so far; and how many weeks there are left in the month.

# Create the Calendar

## Directions

1. Reproduce each pattern onto the suggested paper (see "Calendar Components").

2. Provide each student with the calendar components, and with your class complete the following steps:

3. Cut out the pattern pieces.

4. Glue the poem to the front of the T-shirt.

5. Glue the T-shirt pattern to the bottom of the page (above the actual calendar), as shown. Fan-fold the skin-toned strips; glue one to each of the T-shirt sleeves. Glue and/or staple the hands to the end of the "arms."

6. Glue the head in place and add the yarn "hair."

7. Glue the heart in the palm of one of the hands. (Show students how they can tape the calendar on the wall and tape the hands extended on either side.)

## Calendar Components

### Each student will need:

• 1 June Calendar affixed to the bottom half of a 12" x 18" piece of light-green construction paper

• 1 poem

• 1 T-shirt (reproduce on any color except for green)

• 1 head; 1 set of hands (reproduce on paper of similar color to student's skin color)

• 1 heart (reproduce on pink or red paper)

• yarn to create hair (cut various lengths from a variety of colors for students to choose from)

• 2 strips of skin colored construction paper, 1" x 18" (provide different skin-toned colored papers)

**My Dad**

How do I measure my love for you—
In inches, or yards, or miles?
I could measure with rulers or
yardsticks too,
But I'd rather use hugs and smiles.

**My Dad**

How do I measure my love for you—
In inches, or yards, or miles?
I could measure with rulers or
yardsticks too,
But I'd rather use hugs and smiles.

**My Dad**

How do I measure my love for you—
In inches, or yards, or miles?
I could measure with rulers or
yardsticks too,
But I'd rather use hugs and smiles.

**My Dad**

How do I measure my love for you—
In inches, or yards, or miles?
I could measure with rulers or
yardsticks too,
But I'd rather use hugs and smiles.

**My Dad**

How do I measure my love for you—
In inches, or yards, or miles?
I could measure with rulers or
yardsticks too,
But I'd rather use hugs and smiles.

**My Dad**

How do I measure my love for you—
In inches, or yards, or miles?
I could measure with rulers or
yardsticks too,
But I'd rather use hugs and smiles.

**My Dad**

How do I measure my love for you—
In inches, or yards, or miles?
I could measure with rulers or
yardsticks too,
But I'd rather use hugs and smiles.

**My Dad**

How do I measure my love for you—
In inches, or yards, or miles?
I could measure with rulers or
yardsticks too,
But I'd rather use hugs and smiles.

— Reproducible Page —

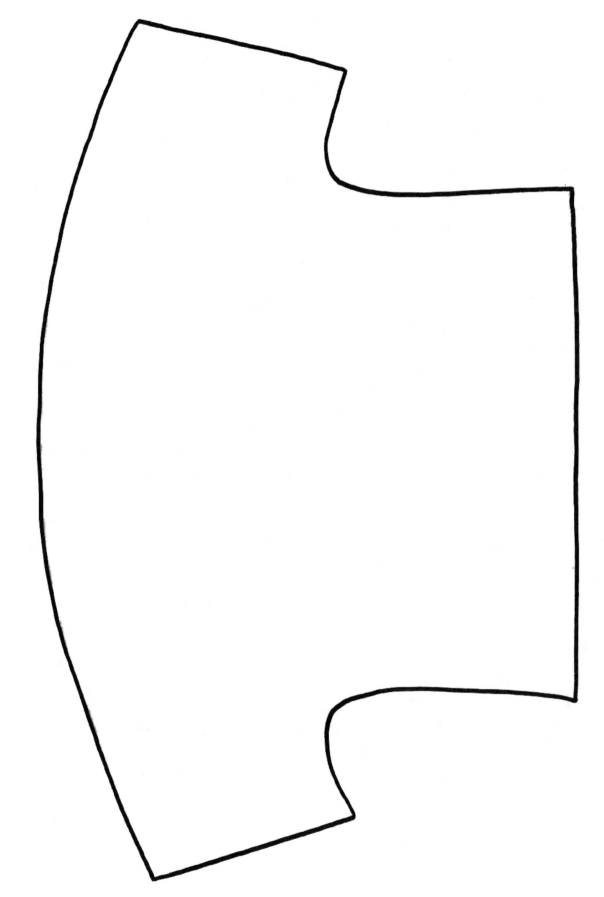

## **Shirt Pattern**

# Head and Hand Patterns

— Reproducible Page —

## Heart Pattern

- *Summer Stinks* by Marty Kelly
- *Summer* by Patricia Whitehouse
- *One Hot Summer Day* by Nina Crews

## School Is Out

The year is over,
School is out,
Summer is here,
We'll laugh and shout.

Hooray for us!
We're on our way.
It's time for us to
Play, play, play!

## ACTIVITIES ➤

### SKILL CODES

## A, C, G, I

## Reasoning

- Ask students the following questions: "How many days have we spent in school this year? How can we solve this equation? What tools can we use? (calendar; "days in school" number line, etc.) Let's solve for the answer. How can we check our work?"
- Now ask students these questions: "How many days will we have of summer vacation? How can we figure this out? What tools can we use?"

## List and Graph (younger grades)

- Have each student make a list of the top five activities of the school year. Direct them to list these activities by how much they liked the activity. For example, the first activity on each list should be her/his favorite (list as #1).
- Allow students to share.
- Compare and contrast the activities.
- Make a graph listing the top 10 activities as determined by the entire class.

## List and Graph (older grades)

- Have each student make a list of the top 10 activities of the school year.
- List the activities on the board in chronological order.

- Now call for a show of hands for each activity to determine which was the majority favorite (list as #1), their second favorite (list as #2), etc.
- Compare and contrast the activities.
- Make a graph listing the top 10 activities.

## Create the Calendar

# Directions

1. Reproduce each pattern onto the suggested paper (see "Calendar Components").

2. Provide each student with the calendar components, and with your class complete the following steps:

3. Cut out the pattern pieces.

4. Glue the black paper on the frame.

5. Glue the framed black paper on the calendar toward the left-hand side.

6. Glue the poem on the lower right-hand corner of the page (above the actual calendar).

7. Draw a smiley face on the yellow circle. Glue the smiley face inside the upper left-hand corner of the frame.

8. Using white chalk, colored pencil, or crayon, have the students write "School Is Out!" on the black paper. (To prevent chalk from smudging, spray clear acrylic fixative or hair spray over the writing.)

## Calendar Components

## Each student will need:

- 1 June Calendar affixed to the bottom half of a piece of 12" x 18" piece of light-blue construction paper
- 1 poem
- 1 smiley face (reproduce on yellow construction paper and have students draw actual face)
- 1 frame (reproduce on brown or tan paper)
- 1 piece of black construction paper (7½" x 6½")

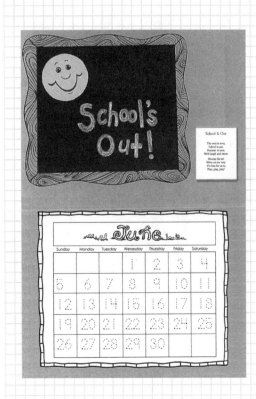

### School Is Out

The year is over,
School is out,
Summer is here,
We'll laugh and shout.

Hooray for us!
We're on our way.
It's time for us to
Play, play, play!

### School Is Out

The year is over,
School is out,
Summer is here,
We'll laugh and shout.

Hooray for us!
We're on our way.
It's time for us to
Play, play, play!

### School Is Out

The year is over,
School is out,
Summer is here,
We'll laugh and shout.

Hooray for us!
We're on our way.
It's time for us to
Play, play, play!

### School Is Out

The year is over,
School is out,
Summer is here,
We'll laugh and shout.

Hooray for us!
We're on our way.
It's time for us to
Play, play, play!

### School Is Out

The year is over,
School is out,
Summer is here,
We'll laugh and shout.

Hooray for us!
We're on our way.
It's time for us to
Play, play, play!

### School Is Out

The year is over,
School is out,
Summer is here,
We'll laugh and shout.

Hooray for us!
We're on our way.
It's time for us to
Play, play, play!

### School Is Out

The year is over,
School is out,
Summer is here,
We'll laugh and shout.

Hooray for us!
We're on our way.
It's time for us to
Play, play, play!

### School Is Out

The year is over,
School is out,
Summer is here,
We'll laugh and shout.

Hooray for us!
We're on our way.
It's time for us to
Play, play, play!

### School Is Out

The year is over,
School is out,
Summer is here,
We'll laugh and shout.

Hooray for us!
We're on our way.
It's time for us to
Play, play, play!

— Reproducible Page —

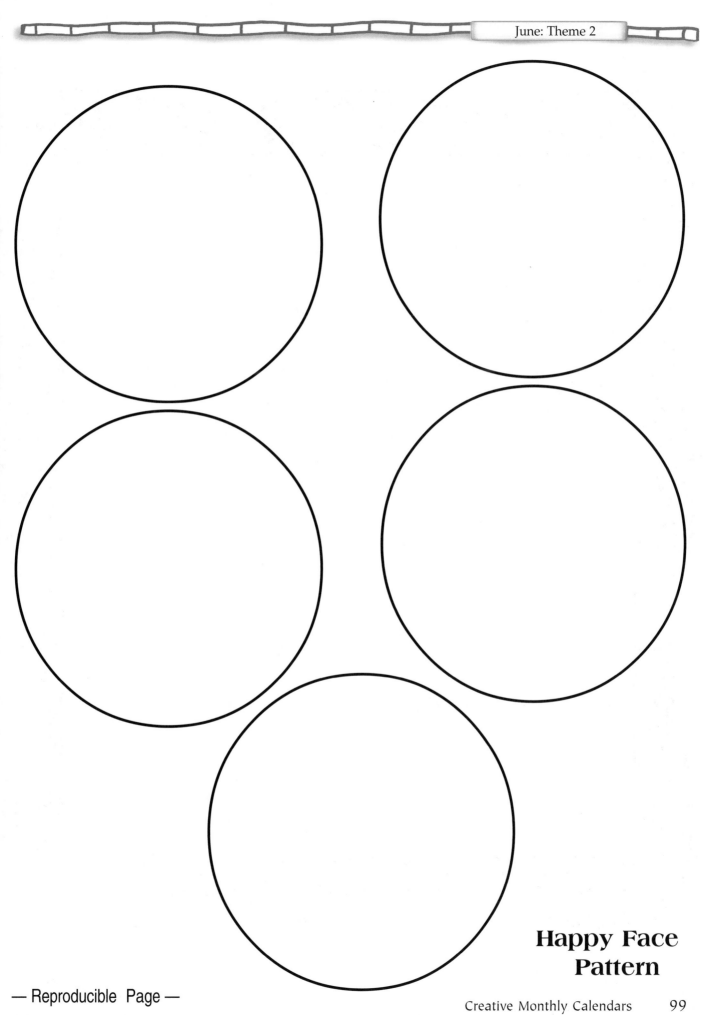

June: Theme 2

**Happy Face Pattern**

# Frame Pattern

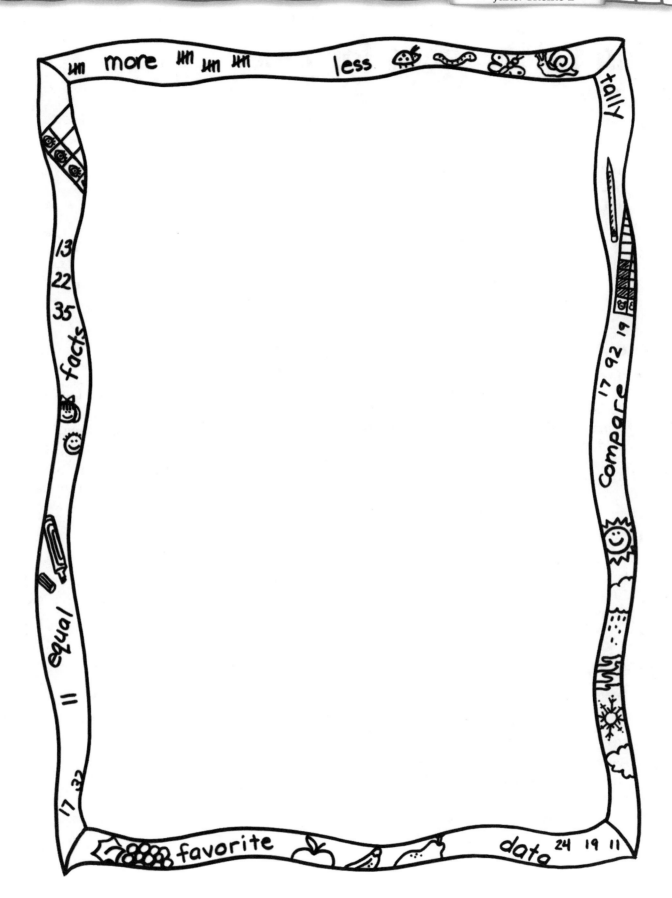

## Frame Pattern

# Fun Celebrations for June

## June 1

This is the first day of National Fresh Fruit and Vegetable Month. Ask your students if they know the difference between a fruit and a vegetable. Cut open different fruits and vegetables. Students will notice that all fruits have seeds. That's right—tomatoes and peppers are fruits! Encourage your students to eat several helpings of fresh fruits and vegetables every day.

## June 2

Today is Paul Galdone's birthday. Galdone is the author of many popular children's stories, including *Henny Penny*, *The Little Red Hen*, and *The Gingerbread Boy*. So pull those Galdone books off the shelf and . . . read, read fast as you can. Can't stop us—we're the kindergarten clan!

## June 9

Happy Birthday, Donald Duck! Yes, this favorite quacker was created on this day in 1934. Celebrate by watching your favorite Donald cartoon.

## June 14

Today is Flag Day. Do your students know that the 13 stripes stand for the original 13 colonies? Or that the 50 stars stand for the 50 states of the union? The color red represents courage, the color white for liberty, and the color blue for justice? Take a moment to honor our flag and all it symbolizes. Say the Pledge of Allegiance.

## June 18

This is National Splurge Day, so go ahead and indulge on something wonderful!

## June 19

Don't forget to wish Garfield a happy birthday today. This lasagna-loving cat was born on this day in 1978. In Garfield's honor, make lasagna for dinner tonight. Yummy!

## June 27

On this day in 1859 Mildred J. Hill, a school teacher, wrote the song "Good Morning to All." This song was altered in 1924 to "Happy Birthday to You." Mildred Hill died in 1916 without knowing her melody would become one of the most popular in the world.

## June 29

Antoine de Saint-Exupéry was born this day in 1900. He is the author of many works, including *The Little Prince*.

# Theme 1:
# The Fourth of July

The Fourth of July

The fireworks, they light the sky,
We eat hot dogs and apple pie.
Our nation's anthem we will sing,
Let the sounds of freedom ring.
Citizens, stand brave and true,
America, we love you!

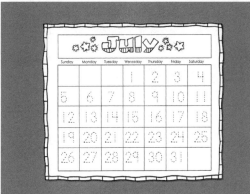

At the Beach

Listen to the ocean roar
As waves crash down upon the shore.
All the children are at play.
Castles rise . . . then wash away,
When the sun fades from the sky,
It's time to pack and say goodbye.

# Theme 2:
# At the Beach

# Literature LINK

- *Hats Off for the Fourth of July* by Harriet Ziefert
- *The Fourth of July Story* by Alice Palgliesh
- *The Star-Spangled Banner* by Peter Spier
- *America the Beautiful* by Katharine Lee Bates

## The Fourth of July

Fireworks light up the sky;
We eat hot dogs and apple pie.
Our nation's anthem we will sing;
Let the sounds of freedom ring.
Citizens, stand brave and true;
America, we love you!

## ACTIVITIES ➤

### SKILL CODES

## A, C, I, J

# Ordinal Position Guessing Game

- Select one student to serve as the game leader; select one student to serve as the player.
- Ask the leader to arrange six cups (party supply stores stock inexpensive cups with patriotic and other designs and colors) in a row, with labels (first, second, third, fourth, fifth) facing the players.
- Have the player close her/his eyes, and ask the leader to hide a small paper flag, an eraser, or some other object underneath one of the cups.
- The player now guesses the location by saying: "I think the flag is hidden under the third cup."
- With the entire class, count together as the teacher/leader points to the cups: "First, second, third." The teacher then lifts the third cup. If the player guessed correctly s/he becomes the leader and chooses another player. If the player guessed incorrectly, s/he may make another guess and you begin the process all over again, continuing on until the object has been found.

# Line Up

- Use ordinal numbers to denote positions as you dismiss students: "Barbara may line up first, John second, Trisha third. . . ."

## Create the Calendar

# Directions

1. Reproduce each pattern onto the suggested paper (see "Calendar Components").

2. Measure, then cut paper strips.

3. Provide each student with the calendar components, and with your class complete the following steps:

4. Cut out the pattern piece.

5. Glue the blue rectangle in the upper left-hand corner, matching the corner edge for edge.

6. Using the dots as guides, make 50 stars on the blue rectangle in any one of the following ways:
   - Affix self-stick foil stars to each dot.
   - Put a dab of glue on each dot and then sprinkle on clear or white glitter.
   - Put a dab of glitter glue on each dot.
   - Use a cotton swab dipped in white paint to dab on each dot.

7. Add the red stripes by first gluing one 6½" strip on the top edge of the paper. Continue gluing stripes as shown using the first stripe as a guide. Leave a ¾" space between each stripe.

8. Glue the poem in the lower right-hand corner.

## Calendar Components

## Each student will need:

- 1 July Calendar affixed to the bottom half of a 12" x 18" piece of white construction paper

- 1 poem

- 7 paper strips (cut strips from red construction paper: 4 measuring 6½" x ½" and 3 measuring 12" x ½")

- rectangle (reproduce on blue paper; dots indicate where to place stars)

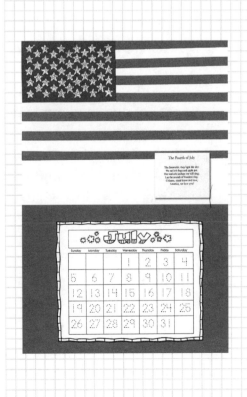

## The Fourth of July

Fireworks light up the sky;
We eat hot dogs and apple pie.
Our nation's anthem we will sing;
Let the sounds of freedom ring.
Citizens, stand brave and true;
America, we love you!

## The Fourth of July

Fireworks light up the sky;
We eat hot dogs and apple pie.
Our nation's anthem we will sing;
Let the sounds of freedom ring.
Citizens, stand brave and true;
America, we love you!

## The Fourth of July

Fireworks light up the sky;
We eat hot dogs and apple pie.
Our nation's anthem we will sing;
Let the sounds of freedom ring.
Citizens, stand brave and true;
America, we love you!

## The Fourth of July

Fireworks light up the sky;
We eat hot dogs and apple pie.
Our nation's anthem we will sing;
Let the sounds of freedom ring.
Citizens, stand brave and true;
America, we love you!

## The Fourth of July

Fireworks light up the sky;
We eat hot dogs and apple pie.
Our nation's anthem we will sing;
Let the sounds of freedom ring.
Citizens, stand brave and true;
America, we love you!

## The Fourth of July

Fireworks light up the sky;
We eat hot dogs and apple pie.
Our nation's anthem we will sing;
Let the sounds of freedom ring.
Citizens, stand brave and true;
America, we love you!

## The Fourth of July

Fireworks light up the sky;
We eat hot dogs and apple pie.
Our nation's anthem we will sing;
Let the sounds of freedom ring.
Citizens, stand brave and true;
America, we love you!

## The Fourth of July

Fireworks light up the sky;
We eat hot dogs and apple pie.
Our nation's anthem we will sing;
Let the sounds of freedom ring.
Citizens, stand brave and true;
America, we love you!

— Reproducible Page —

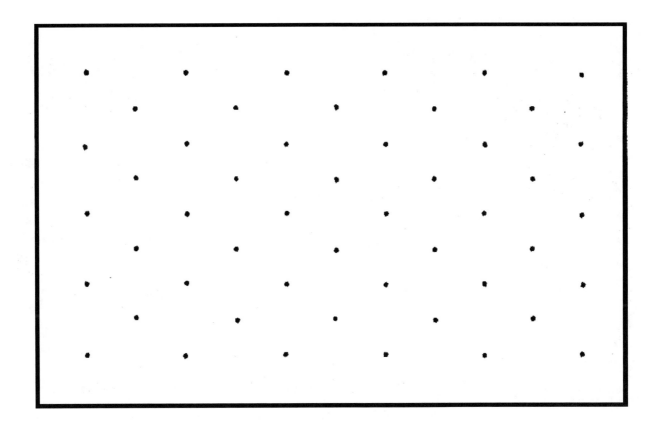

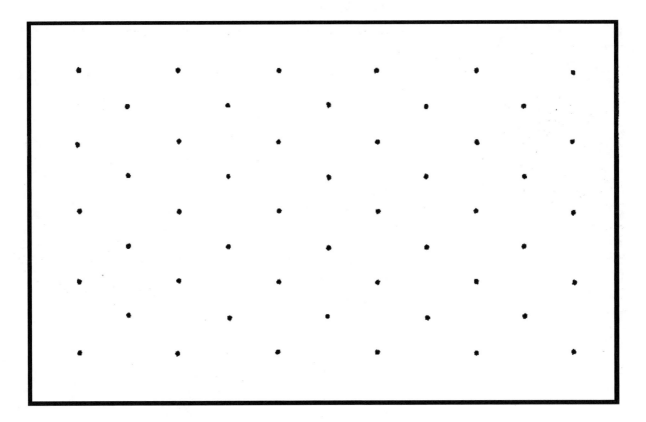

# Rectangle Pattern for Stars

# Literature LINK

- *On My Beach There Are Many Pebbles* by Leo Lionni
- *Beach Day* by Karen Roosa
- *10,000 White Horses* by Betsy B. Lee
- *At the Beach* by Huy Voun Lee

## At the Beach

Listen to the ocean roar
As waves crash down upon the shore;
All the children are at play,
Castles rise . . . then wash away.
When the sun fades from the sky
It's time to pack and say goodbye.

## ACTIVITIES ➤

## SKILL CODES

## A, C, D, I

# Seashell Addition/Subtraction

- Place sand in a box top or tray. Use seashells as manipulatives.
- Create addition and subtraction sentences such as:

"There are five (5) seashells on the beach. Isabella found one and took it home. How many seashells are left on the beach?" (5 - 1 = 4)

"There were three (3) seashells on the beach. Then a wave crashed down and dropped three (3) more on the beach. How many seashells are on the beach?" (3 + 3 = 6)

# Seashell Patterns

- Using either real seashells or photocopied shell patterns, allow the children to create patterns. Begin with simple ABABAB patterns and then progress to more complex patterns.

## Create the Calendar

# Directions

1. Reproduce each pattern onto the suggested paper (see "Calendar Components").

2. Provide each student with the calendar components, and with your class complete the following steps:

3. Cut out the pattern pieces.

4. Glue the poem in the upper left-hand corner.

5. Glue the sun pattern to the top center of the page (above the actual calendar). The sun will extend above the top edge.

6. Have students tear or cut a wavy line along the length of one side of their piece of dark-blue paper to look like the ocean. Glue this piece in place at the bottom of the calendar.

7. Have students tear or cut a wavy line along one length of the tan paper to resemble the sand. Glue this piece on top of the "ocean," matching up the bottom edges. Optional: You may wish to add a wide row of glue along the edge of the tan paper, and then sprinkle real sand on the glue to resemble the beach.

8. Finally, have students arrange and then glue the shells along the bottom of the "sand." Decorate the shells with patterns of glitter glue to add dimension.

## Calendar Components

### Each student will need:

- 1 July Calendar affixed to the bottom half of a 12" x 18" piece of light-blue construction paper

- 1 poem

- 1 sun

- a variety of seashells (reproduce on paper, various colors)

- 1 piece of dark-blue paper (4½" x 12")

- 1 piece of tan paper (2½" x 12")

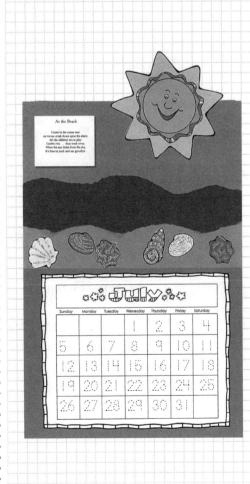

## At the Beach

Listen to the ocean roar
As waves crash down upon the shore;
All the children are at play,
Castles rise . . . then wash away.
When the sun fades from the sky
It's time to pack and say goodbye.

## At the Beach

Listen to the ocean roar
As waves crash down upon the shore;
All the children are at play,
Castles rise . . . then wash away.
When the sun fades from the sky
It's time to pack and say goodbye.

## At the Beach

Listen to the ocean roar
As waves crash down upon the shore;
All the children are at play,
Castles rise . . . then wash away.
When the sun fades from the sky
It's time to pack and say goodbye.

## At the Beach

Listen to the ocean roar
As waves crash down upon the shore;
All the children are at play,
Castles rise . . . then wash away.
When the sun fades from the sky
It's time to pack and say goodbye.

## At the Beach

Listen to the ocean roar
As waves crash down upon the shore;
All the children are at play,
Castles rise . . . then wash away.
When the sun fades from the sky
It's time to pack and say goodbye.

## At the Beach

Listen to the ocean roar
As waves crash down upon the shore;
All the children are at play,
Castles rise . . . then wash away.
When the sun fades from the sky
It's time to pack and say goodbye.

— Reproducible Page —

## **Sun Pattern**

# Seashell Patterns

## Seashell Patterns

# Fun Celebrations for July

## July 1

- The Philadelphia Zoological Society, the first U.S. zoo, opened on this day in 1874. Why not visit a zoo in your home state today.

- Today is also the first day of National Hot Dog Month. Plan a barbeque, complete with salads and yummy desserts!

## July 3

Today is National Stay Out of the Sun Day. Discuss the importance of skin protection and plan some fun indoor activities—wear zany hats and sunglasses *inside*.

## July 4

"America the Beautiful" was published to celebrate Independence Day, which marks the anniversary of the adoption of the Declaration of Independence by the Continental Congress in 1776. Sing in celebration of the Fourth of July today, and don't forget to watch the fireworks!

## Third Sunday in July

The third Sunday in July is National Ice Cream Day. Visit your local dairy or learn how ice cream is made. Of course, the day wouldn't be complete without enjoying at least one scoop of ice cream. Teachers, if you're part of a year-round or summer-school program, graph your student's favorite ice cream flavors. Which flavor is most popular?

## July 20

Today is Moon Day—a great day to learn all about the moon and the astronauts who have landed on it.

## July 27

This is National Parents' Day. Today is a day to reflect on all the wonderful things caregivers do for children. Honor those who strengthen the todays and tomorrows of our communities, by inviting them to a classroom tea or social.

## July 31

Happy Birthday, J.K. Rowling and Harry Potter! Author J.K. Rowling gave Harry the same birthday as her own.

# August

## Theme 1:
## Summer Sun

## Theme 2:
## Picnic

# Literature LINK

- *The Sun* by Niki Walker
- *Sun Up, Sun Down* by Gail Gibbons
- *Sun* by Susan Canizares
- *Sun and Moon* by Marcus Pfister

## Summer Sun*

First, the sun pops up to say,
"Hello! to you, my brand new day."

Second, the sun shines wide and bright,
"Wake up! Wake up! It is daylight."

Third, I shade my eyes to see
The new day that's begun for me.

Fourth, I wash and dress and brush
And do my chores without a fuss.

Fifth, I go outside to play
On a sunny Saturday.

Sixth, I watch the fading light
Then go inside to say, "Good-night."

## ACTIVITIES ➤

### SKILL CODES

## A, C, I

## Time

- Use the art sun clock pattern to create enough clocks for individual students to use during math group instruction.

- Laminate the clock and hands so they can be used again next year.

- Use a hole-punch to punch a hole through the center of the clock and through the laminated clock hands, where indicated. Use a brad to fasten the clock hands to the clock.

- Provide each student with a clock and call out the time to the hour. Have the students move the hands of their clock to show the time.

- When students have moved the hands into position, ask them to hold up the clocks so you can check their results. Continue on, progressing to time to the half-hour and quarter-hour.

- Have students demonstrate time knowledge on the clocks in response to questions. For example, ask questions such as: "Show me the time that school starts each morning. Show me the time that we go to lunch. What time do we go home from school?"

* Finger-Play

## Calendar Components

### Each student will need:

- 1 August Calendar affixed to the bottom half of a 12" x 18" piece of dark-blue construction paper
- 1 poem
- 1 set of clock hands (reproduce on orange construction paper)
- 1 sun face (reproduce on yellow construction paper)
- 1 sun ray (reproduce on orange construction paper)
- 1 brad (brass fastener)
- optional: chalk or colored pencils, for detail

## Create the Calendar

# Directions

1. Reproduce each pattern onto the suggested paper (see "Calendar Components").

2. Provide each student with the calendar components, and with your class complete the following steps:

3. Cut out the pattern pieces.

4. Glue the poem in the lower left-hand corner of the page (above the actual calendar).

5. Model how the pattern pieces should be assembled.

6. Glue the yellow face onto the orange rays.

7. Attach the hands of the clock with a brad.

8. Glue the completed clock on the calendar as shown.

9. If desired, use chalk or colored pencil to color in the cheeks and eyes on the sun face.

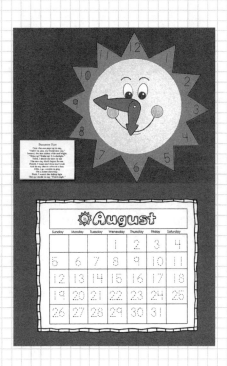

## Summer Sun

First, the sun pops up to say,
"Hello! to you, my brand new day."
Second, the sun shines wide and bright,
"Wake up! Wake up! It is daylight."
Third, I shade my eyes to see
The new day that's begun for me.
Fourth, I wash and dress and brush
And do my chores without a fuss.
Fifth, I go outside to play
On a sunny Saturday.
Sixth, I watch the fading light
Then go inside to say, "Good-night."

## Summer Sun

First, the sun pops up to say,
"Hello! to you, my brand new day."
Second, the sun shines wide and bright,
"Wake up! Wake up! It is daylight."
Third, I shade my eyes to see
The new day that's begun for me.
Fourth, I wash and dress and brush
And do my chores without a fuss.
Fifth, I go outside to play
On a sunny Saturday.
Sixth, I watch the fading light
Then go inside to say, "Good-night."

## Summer Sun

First, the sun pops up to say,
"Hello! to you, my brand new day."
Second, the sun shines wide and bright,
"Wake up! Wake up! It is daylight."
Third, I shade my eyes to see
The new day that's begun for me.
Fourth, I wash and dress and brush
And do my chores without a fuss.
Fifth, I go outside to play
On a sunny Saturday.
Sixth, I watch the fading light
Then go inside to say, "Good-night."

## Summer Sun

First, the sun pops up to say,
"Hello! to you, my brand new day."
Second, the sun shines wide and bright,
"Wake up! Wake up! It is daylight."
Third, I shade my eyes to see
The new day that's begun for me.
Fourth, I wash and dress and brush
And do my chores without a fuss.
Fifth, I go outside to play
On a sunny Saturday.
Sixth, I watch the fading light
Then go inside to say, "Good-night."

## Summer Sun

First, the sun pops up to say,
"Hello! to you, my brand new day."
Second, the sun shines wide and bright,
"Wake up! Wake up! It is daylight."
Third, I shade my eyes to see
The new day that's begun for me.
Fourth, I wash and dress and brush
And do my chores without a fuss.
Fifth, I go outside to play
On a sunny Saturday.
Sixth, I watch the fading light
Then go inside to say, "Good-night."

## Summer Sun

First, the sun pops up to say,
"Hello! to you, my brand new day."
Second, the sun shines wide and bright,
"Wake up! Wake up! It is daylight."
Third, I shade my eyes to see
The new day that's begun for me.
Fourth, I wash and dress and brush
And do my chores without a fuss.
Fifth, I go outside to play
On a sunny Saturday.
Sixth, I watch the fading light
Then go inside to say, "Good-night."

— Reproducible Page —

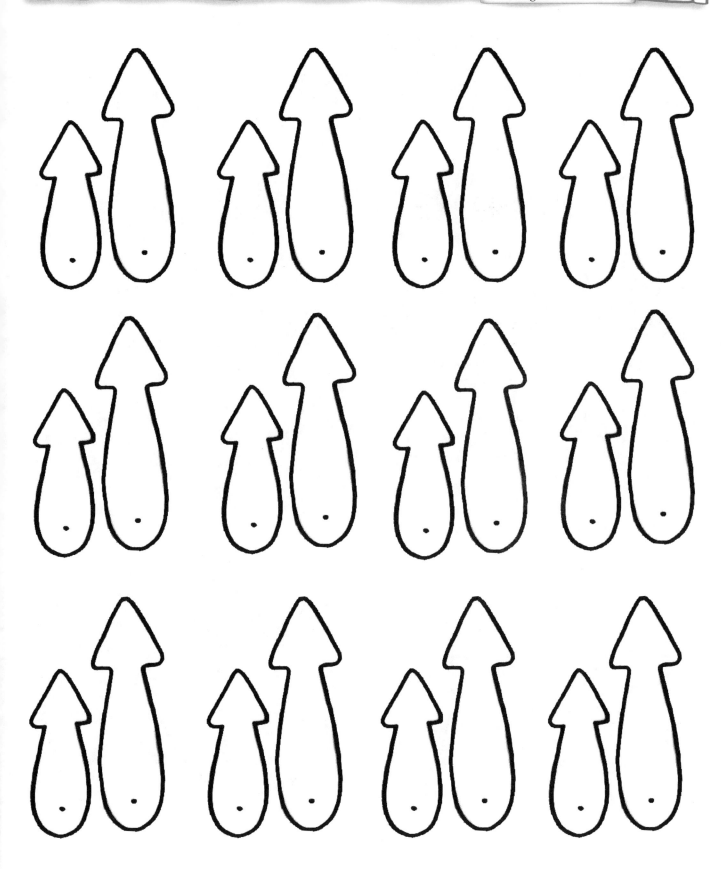

## Sun Clock Hands Pattern

## Sun Clock Face Pattern

## Sun Clock Pattern

Creative Monthly Calendars    121

# Literature LINK

- *A Picnic in October* by Eve Bunting
- *We're Going on a Picnic* by Pat Hutchins
- *The Teddy Bears' Picnic* by Jimmy Kennedy
- *Picnic* by Mick Inkpen
- *One Hundred Hungry Ants* by Bonnie MacKain

## Picnic

In a basket packed with care
You'll find plates and silverware;
Sandwiches, pickles, potato chips;
Vegetables, fruits, and yummy dips.
On a cloth of red and white
A picnic for us,
O! What a delight!

## ACTIVITIES ➤

### SKILL CODES

## A, C, D, I

# The Ants Go Marching

- Sing the song "The Ants Go Marching," or read the book.
- Use plastic ants to demonstrate marching one by one, two by two, three by three, and so on.

# Ants on a Log

- Give each child a celery stalk filled with peanut butter or cream cheese and a small cup of raisins (a.k.a., the ants).
- Make addition or subtraction sentences using the ants on a log as a manipulative. For example: "There are no (0) ants on my log. Two (2) ants have decided to walk on my log and stop to take a rest." (0 + 2 = 2)
- After practicing several addition/subtraction sentences, eat your ant log.

# Ant Patterns

- Reproduce ant pattern onto red, brown, and gray paper.
- Laminate and cut apart.
- Have students make patterns using the different colored ants.

## Create the Calendar

# Directions

1. Reproduce each pattern onto the suggested paper (see "Calendar Components").

2. Provide each student with the calendar components, and with your class complete the following steps:

3. Cut out the pattern pieces.

4. Glue the squares in place around the outside of the page (above the actual calendar). Be sure to place them on the edge and allow a distance of one inch between each square. For younger students, provide a piece of cardboard (one-inch wide) to use as a guide.

5. Cut out the remaining calendar pieces. Glue (or staple) them in place as shown.

6. Glue the poem in the center of the plate.

7. Glue on the ants. You may wish to have the students attach multiple ants.

## Calendar Components

### Each student will need:

• 1 August Calendar affixed to the bottom half of a 12" x 18" piece of red construction paper

• 1 poem

• 1 plate; 1 napkin (reproduce on white paper)

• 1 set of flatware; 1 set of ants (reproduce on gray paper)

• 22 one-inch squares for table-cloth border (cut from white paper)

Please note: You may choose to use a real paper plate, napkin, and plastic flatware rather than use the paper patterns.

**Picnic**

In a basket packed with care
You'll find plates and silverware;
Sandwiches, pickles, potato chips;
Vegetables, fruits, and yummy dips.
On a cloth of red and white
A picnic for us,
O! What a delight!

**Picnic**

In a basket packed with care
You'll find plates and silverware;
Sandwiches, pickles, potato chips;
Vegetables, fruits, and yummy dips.
On a cloth of red and white
A picnic for us,
O! What a delight!

**Picnic**

In a basket packed with care
You'll find plates and silverware;
Sandwiches, pickles, potato chips;
Vegetables, fruits, and yummy dips.
On a cloth of red and white
A picnic for us,
O! What a delight!

**Picnic**

In a basket packed with care
You'll find plates and silverware;
Sandwiches, pickles, potato chips;
Vegetables, fruits, and yummy dips.
On a cloth of red and white
A picnic for us,
O! What a delight!

**Picnic**

In a basket packed with care
You'll find plates and silverware;
Sandwiches, pickles, potato chips;
Vegetables, fruits, and yummy dips.
On a cloth of red and white
A picnic for us,
O! What a delight!

**Picnic**

In a basket packed with care
You'll find plates and silverware;
Sandwiches, pickles, potato chips;
Vegetables, fruits, and yummy dips.
On a cloth of red and white
A picnic for us,
O! What a delight!

— Reproducible Page —

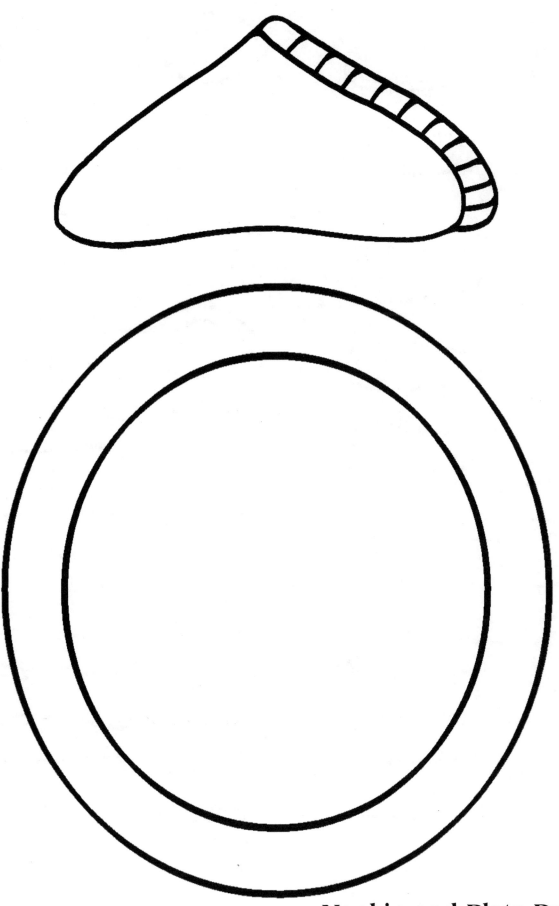

## Napkin and Plate Patterns

# Utensil Patterns

— Reproducible Page —

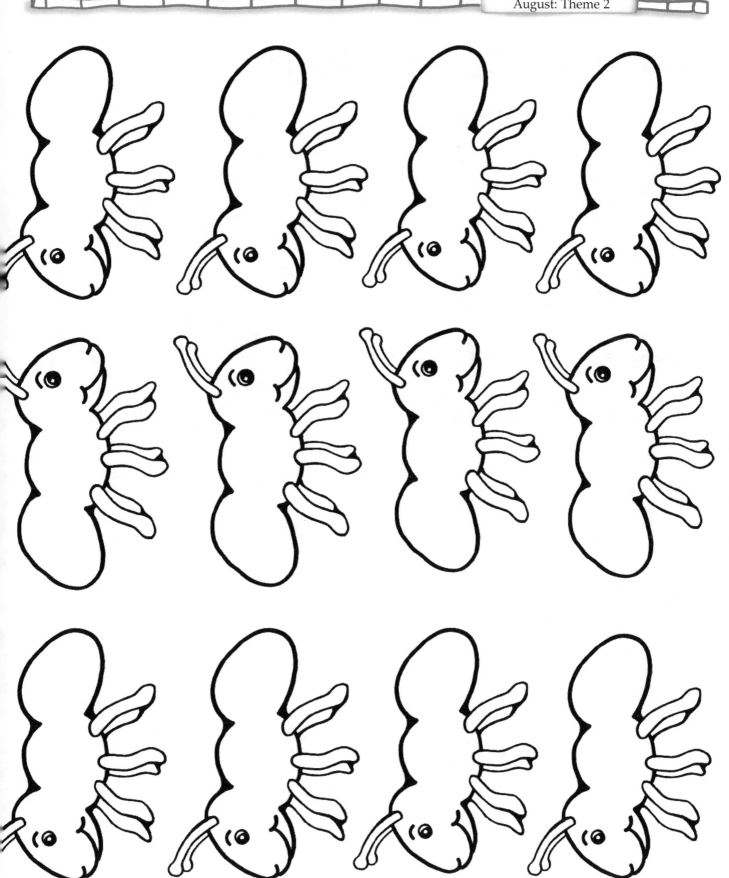

**Ant Patterns**

# Fun Celebrations for August

## First Full Week of August

- The first full week of August is National Smile Week. Try to greet everyone with a smile this week (it is said a smile can be quite contagious!)

- This is also International Clown Week. Consider inviting a clown to visit your summer class or summer party. Children might also have fun dressing up as clowns.

## August 1

This is the first day of Family Fun Month and National Inventors' Month. Invent some ways to have a whole month of family fun!

## August 4

Today is National Sisters' Day. If you have a sister, let her know how much she means to you today (and every day!)

## August 11

The Rugrats premiered on this date in 1991. This is also Popcorn Festival time. Take a break, pop some corn, and watch a little Rugrats today.

## August 19

Today is National Aviation Day. Aviation and its history are fascinating, so why not take a trip to the nearest airport, aviation museum, or air show today.

## August 22

Today is Be an Angel Day. Think of something nice you can do for someone else, and then do it!

## August 26

Today is Women's Equality Day. Share with students that women did not always have the rights and liberties we have today, and discuss with them what women had to do to gain these rights.

# September

## Theme 1:
## Back to School

## Theme 2:
## Apples

# Literature LINK

- *Miss Bindergarten Gets Ready for Kindergarten* by Joseph Slate
- *Countdown to Kindergarten* by Alison McGhee
- *First Day Jitters* by Julie Danneberg
- *Tom Goes to Kindergarten* by Margaret Wild

## Back to School

The School bell is ringing,
Children are singing,
We're on our way
To school today!

Our shoes are new,
Our lunch boxes too,
So shout, "Hooray!"
We're in school today!

## ACTIVITIES ➤

### SKILL CODES

## A, C, F, I

## Flannel Story Directions:

Use the calendar art patterns to make the pieces for the following story (see full-page story layout on page 132). Cut the pieces from felt to use with a flannel board, or attach laminated paper pieces to self-adhesive magnets for use on a magnetic board. This is meant to be a whole-group activity. Attach the appropriate pieces to the flannel or magnetic board as you read the story to your class (directions are embedded within the story).

*1. Place the red square on the top of the storyboard.*

The square was lonely and felt as if he had nothing to do. Then he saw a pile of shapes that were scattered at the bottom of the hill.

*2. Place all shapes on the bottom portion of the storyboard.*

The red square called out, "Please join me up here. The view is wonderful. I am sure that together we could all find something to do." A large red triangle moved up to the top of the hill, end-over-end, until it came to rest (*its tip pointing toward the sky*) on top of the square.

*3. Place the large red triangle on top of the square.*

The large triangle was quite pleased with himself, and he sighed a contented sigh. All of the other shapes cheered and shouted, "Hooray, can we come play?" One by one the other shapes made their way up the hill. The white rectangle pushed up the hill first and leaned right in front of the red square.

*4. Place the white rectangle on the red square.*

Two blue squares skipped side-by-side up the hill, stopping on either side of the white rectangle.

5. *Place the blue squares on the red rectangle, on either side of the white rectangle.*

The little yellow circle bounced and bounced until she reached the top of the hill. Then she bounced right in front of the white triangle.

6. *Place the yellow circle to the right-center of the white rectangle.*

Little red triangle and little red square hurried to join their friends, and they landed one on top of the other above the red triangle.

7. *Place the small red square on top of the large triangle, overlapping until the bottom corners of the square touch the top edges of the large triangle. Then, add the small triangle to the top, its tip pointing skyward.*

Only one shape remained: It was a little bit round and a little bit pointed—not quite a shape at all. But it made the most beautiful sound as it moved to the top of the hill and came to rest on the little red square.

8. *Place the bell on the small red square.*

And there it began to ring out. And soon children came from all around, and the large red square said, "Yes, I knew we could do something meaningful together."

## Create the Calendar

# Directions

1. Reproduce each pattern onto the suggested paper (see "Calendar Components").

2. Provide each student with the calendar components, and with your class complete the following steps:

3. Cut out the pattern pieces.

4. Model the assembly of the schoolhouse, shape-by-shape, assisting students as needed. Glue on school-house components.

5. Glue the poem on the upper right-hand corner.

6. Optional: Students may paint or color grass along the bottom of the schoolhouse.

7. Optional: One boy pattern; one girl pattern (reproduce on white paper and have students decorate to reflect themselves, or include more than one pattern, to represent classmates).

## Calendar Components

## Each student will need:

- 1 September Calendar affixed to the bottom half of a 12" x 18" piece of light-blue construction paper

- 1 poem

- 2 squares for *windows* (cut from light-blue paper)

- 1 bell (reproduce on yellow paper)

- 1 circle for *doorknob* (reproduce on yellow paper)

- 1 rectangle for *door* (cut from white paper)

- 1 boy pattern; 1 girl pattern (reproduce on white paper)

- 1 large square for *schoolhouse*

- 1 small square for *belltower*

- 2 triangles for *roofs* (reproduce the last 3 bulleted components on red paper)

# FUN WITH SHAPES

A large square was sitting on a hill. It was bright red.

*1. Place the red square on the top of the storyboard.*

The square was lonely and felt as if he had nothing to do. Then he saw a pile of shapes that were scattered at the bottom of the hill.

*2. Place all shapes on the bottom portion of the storyboard.*

The red square called out, "Please join me up here. The view is wonderful. I am sure that together we could all find something to do." A large red triangle moved up to the top of the hill, end-over-end, until it came *(its tip pointing toward the sky)* to rest on top of the square.

*3. Place the large red triangle on top of the square.*

The large triangle was quite pleased with himself, and he sighed a contented sigh. All of the other shapes cheered and shouted, "Hooray, can we come play?" One by one the other shapes made their way up the hill. The white rectangle pushed up the hill first and leaned right in front of the red square.

*4. Place the white rectangle on the red square.*

Two blue squares skipped side-by-side up the hill, stopping on either side of the white rectangle.

*5. Place the blue squares on the red rectangle, on either side of the white rectangle.*

The little yellow circle bounced and bounced until she reached the top of the hill. Then she bounced right in front of the white triangle.

*6. Place the yellow circle to the right-center of the white rectangle.*

Little red triangle and little red square hurried to join their friends, and they landed one on top of the other above the red triangle.

*7. Place the small red square on top of the large triangle, overlapping until the bottom corners of the square touch the top edges of the large triangle. Then, add the small triangle to the top, pointing skyward.*

Only one shape remained: It was a little bit round and a little bit pointed—not quite a shape at all. But it made the most beautiful sound as it moved to the top of the hill and came to rest on the little red square.

*8. Place the bell on the small red square.*

And there it began to ring out. And soon children came from all around, and the large red square said, "Yes, I knew we could do something meaningful together."

— Reproducible Page —

## Back to School

The School bell is ringing,
Children are singing,
We're on our way
To school today!

Our shoes are new,
Our lunch boxes too,
So shout, "Hooray!"
We're in school today!

## Back to School

The School bell is ringing,
Children are singing,
We're on our way
To school today!

Our shoes are new,
Our lunch boxes too,
So shout, "Hooray!"
We're in school today!

## Back to School

The School bell is ringing,
Children are singing,
We're on our way
To school today!

Our shoes are new,
Our lunch boxes too,
So shout, "Hooray!"
We're in school today!

## Back to School

The School bell is ringing,
Children are singing,
We're on our way
To school today!

Our shoes are new,
Our lunch boxes too,
So shout, "Hooray!"
We're in school today!

## Back to School

The School bell is ringing,
Children are singing,
We're on our way
To school today!

Our shoes are new,
Our lunch boxes too,
So shout, "Hooray!"
We're in school today!

## Back to School

The School bell is ringing,
Children are singing,
We're on our way
To school today!

Our shoes are new,
Our lunch boxes too,
So shout, "Hooray!"
We're in school today!

— Reproducible Page —

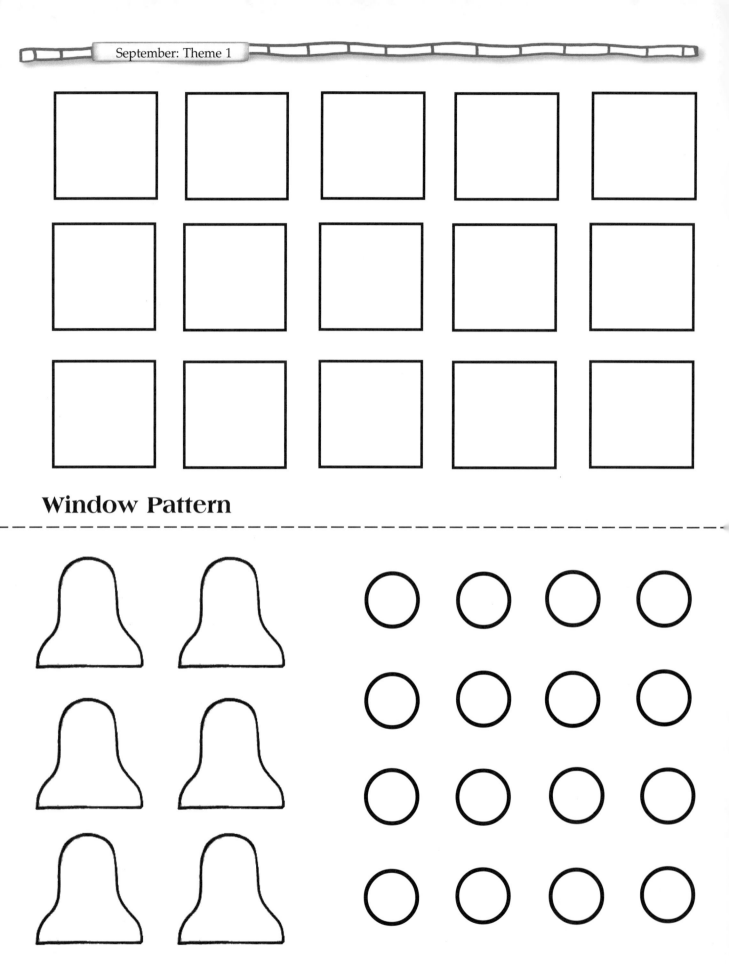

## Window Pattern

## Bell and Doorknob Patterns

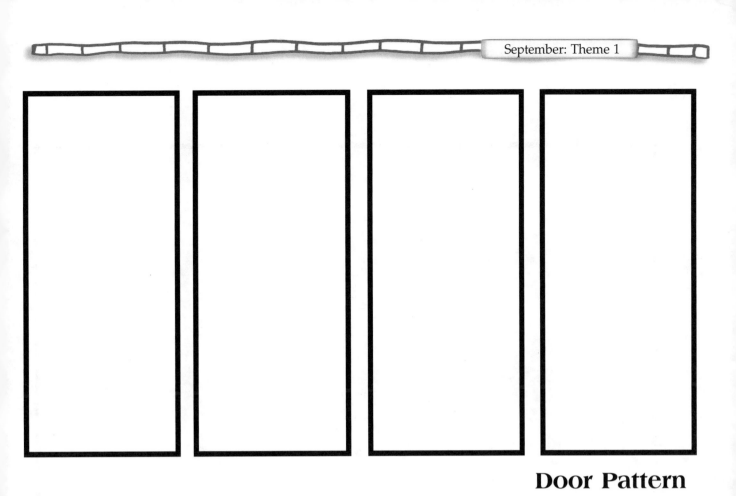

## Door Pattern

## Boy and Girl Patterns

# School House Pattern

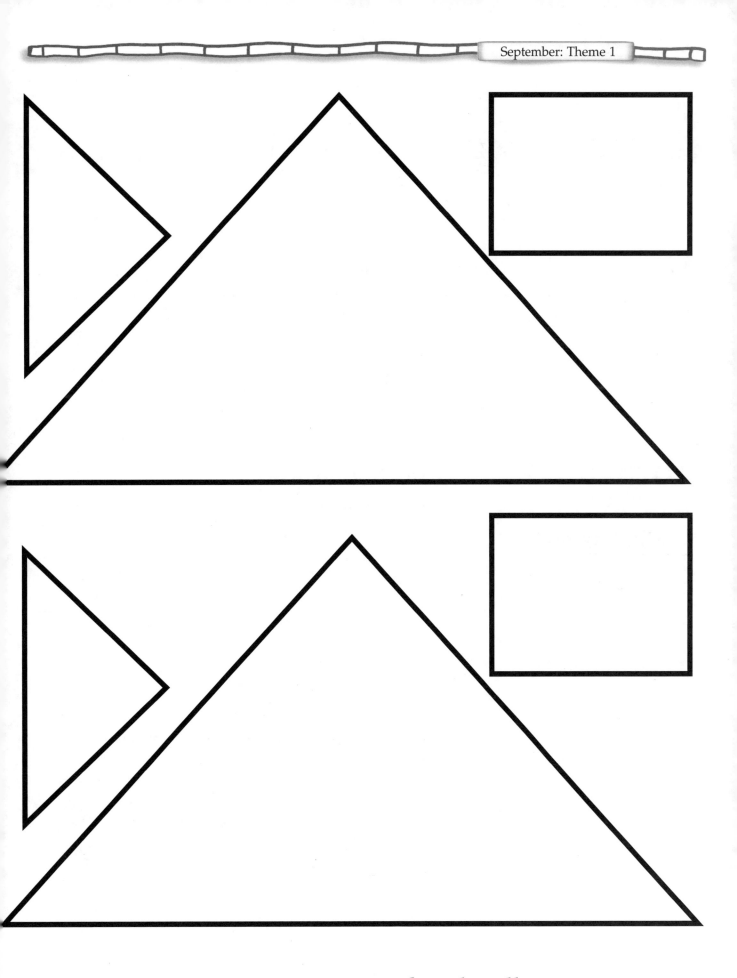

# Roof and Bell Tower Patterns

# Literature LINK

- *The Seasons of Arnold's Apple Tree* by Gail Gibbons
- *Apples, Apples, Apples* by Nancy Elizabeth Wallace
- *Ten Red Apples* by Pat Hutchins

## Apples

Apples round and shiny,
Yellow, red, and green;
Some are small, some are large,
And some are in between.

Apples crisp and crunchy,
Sweet and good to munch;
They smell so fresh and yummy,
I'll have one for my lunch.

## ACTIVITIES ➤

## SKILL CODES

## A, C, E, F, H, I, J,

## "Ordering" Apple

- Photocopy the apple pattern in several different sizes.
- Cut the apples out and laminate.
- Have the students arrange the apples from smallest to largest.

## Apple Pattern

- Reproduce the apple pattern on red, green, and yellow papers.
- Cut out the apples and laminate.
- Have the students create color patterns using the apple cards.

## Apple Graph

- Ask students to predict which apple they will like the best. Ask each student why s/he made that decision.
- Allow each student to have a taste of a red, green, and yellow apple.
- Graph which apple each student liked the most. Which color apple was the most popular? Which was liked the least?

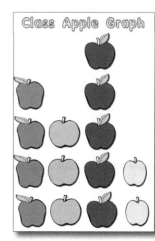
Class Apple Graph

# Bite Estimation with Apples

- Give each student one apple.

- Ask students to make individual predictions as to how many bites it will take to eat their apples. Students should write down their estimates and then begin to eat.

- Instruct students to make one tally mark for each bite they take. How many bites did it take to eat the apple? How close was the original estimate to the actual number of bites taken?

## Create the Calendar

# Directions

1. Reproduce each pattern onto the suggested paper (see "Calendar Components").

2. Provide each student with the calendar components, and with your class complete the following steps:

3. Cut out the pattern pieces.

4. Glue the four-inch tan strips along the length of one nine-inch strip (match edges). Allow it to dry.

5. Cut out the apples and leaves.

6. Color the apples' stems with a brown felt marker.

7. Glue a leaf on some of the apples.

8. Complete the tan basket by weaving the remaining nine-inch strip through the four-inch strips.

9. When spaced correctly, glue the basket to the bottom of the page (above the actual calendar) around the sides and bottom only. Leave the top open so students can slide the apples partially in and glue them in place. Apples should overlap.

10. Glue the poem in the upper right-hand corner of the page.

## Calendar Components

### Each student will need:

- 1 September Calendar affixed to the bottom half of a 12" x 18" piece of light-blue construction paper

- 1 poem

- 3-4 apples (reproduce on red, green, and yellow paper; provide each student with an assortment)

- 1 set of leaves (reproduce on light-green and/or dark-green paper)

- 2 strips of tan paper (1" x 9"); 9 strips of tan paper (1" x 4")

## Apples

Apples round and shiny,
Yellow, red, and green;
Some are small, some are large,
And some are in between.

Apples crisp and crunchy,
Sweet and good to munch;
They smell so fresh and yummy,
I'll have one for my lunch.

## Apples

Apples round and shiny,
Yellow, red, and green;
Some are small, some are large,
And some are in between.

Apples crisp and crunchy,
Sweet and good to munch;
They smell so fresh and yummy,
I'll have one for my lunch.

## Apples

Apples round and shiny,
Yellow, red, and green;
Some are small, some are large,
And some are in between.

Apples crisp and crunchy,
Sweet and good to munch;
They smell so fresh and yummy,
I'll have one for my lunch.

## Apples

Apples round and shiny,
Yellow, red, and green;
Some are small, some are large,
And some are in between.

Apples crisp and crunchy,
Sweet and good to munch;
They smell so fresh and yummy,
I'll have one for my lunch.

## Apples

Apples round and shiny,
Yellow, red, and green;
Some are small, some are large,
And some are in between.

Apples crisp and crunchy,
Sweet and good to munch;
They smell so fresh and yummy,
I'll have one for my lunch.

## Apples

Apples round and shiny,
Yellow, red, and green;
Some are small, some are large,
And some are in between.

Apples crisp and crunchy,
Sweet and good to munch;
They smell so fresh and yummy,
I'll have one for my lunch.

— Reproducible Page —

## Apple Pattern

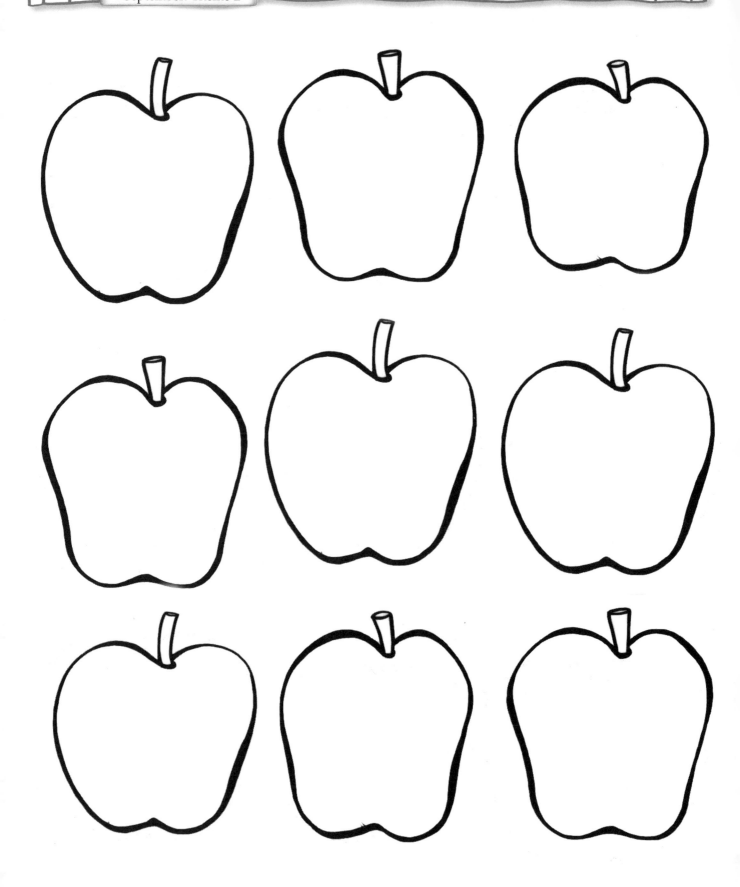

# Apple Pattern

— Reproducible  Page —

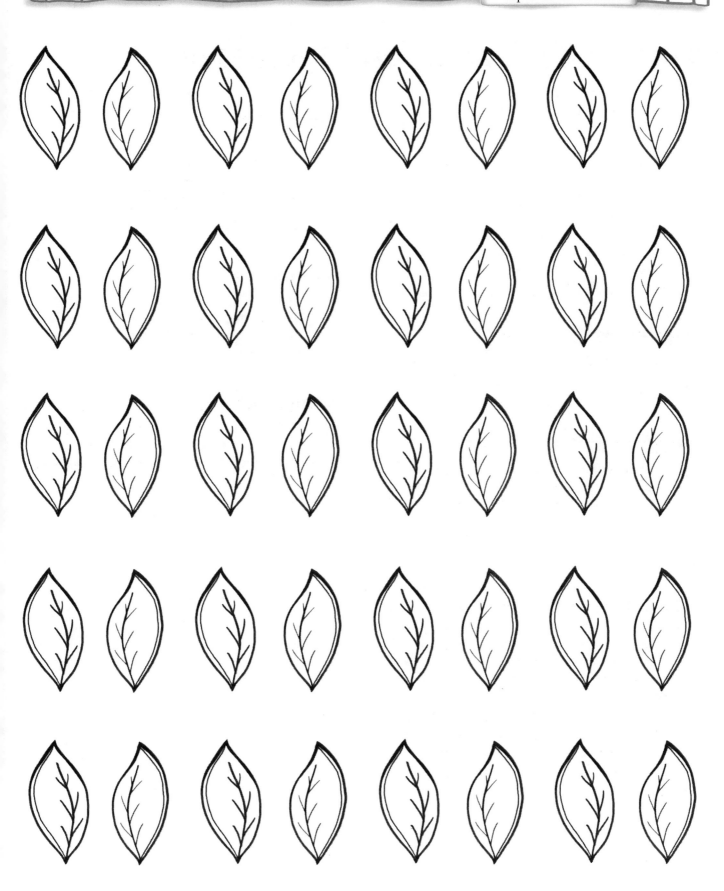

# Apple Leaf Pattern

# Fun Celebrations for September

## September 1

- This is the first day of Children's Good Manners Month. Get the school year off to a great start by reviewing what kinds of behaviors demonstrate good manners.

- This is also National Library Card Sign-Up Month. Plan a trip to the local library and make sure every student has or receives a library card and instructions on how easy it is to check out a book.

## September 2

This is "Be Late for Something Day." Encourage your students to slow down and enjoy life.

## September 8

Today is National Grandparents' Day. Encourage your students to make a greeting card for their grandparents or an elderly loved one. Consider inviting students' grandparents to visit the class and share what life was like when they were in school.

## Second Week of September

- This is Substitute Teacher Appreciation Week. Ask your students to make something special for their favorite substitute teacher. Invite him/her to visit the class for a celebration.

- This is also National Farm Animals' Week. Plan a field trip to a local farm and discuss how important farmers are to our communities.

## September 16

Today is National Play-Doh Day. Make sure you have plenty available for children to use. Ask students to make letters and/or spell their names using Play-Doh. Try making your own Play-Doh with flour, water, cream of tartar, and food coloring.

## September 19

This is National Student Day—Recognize your students' achievements and efforts. Let your students know how wonderful they are.

## September 22

Today is the birthday of the ice cream cone. Ice cream cones were first made of paper. Lucky for us, today they are edible pastry shells.

# October

## Theme 1: Halloween

## Theme 2: Fall Leaves

# Literature LINK

- *The Little Old Lady Who Was Not Afraid of Anything* by Linda Williams
- *The Halloween Parade* by Rosemary Wells
- *Five Little Pumpkins* by Iris van Rynbach
- *On Halloween* by Lark Carrier

## Halloween Surprise

The rafters are creaking,
The hinges are squeaking,
The wind is howling
And dogs are growling;
The windows clatter
(My teeth start to chatter),
Then I hear ring - ring - ring:
"Happy Halloween!"

## ACTIVITIES ➤

### SKILL CODES

## A, B, C, I, K

## Candy Sort

- Give each student a small cup filled with various types of Halloween candy.
- Ask each child to sort the candy into categories.
- When students have finished sorting, they must tell you how many items are in each set and what sorting rule (e.g., shape, color, type of object) they used for classification.

## Matching Sets

- Provide each student with an assortment of Halloween erasers (e.g., ghosts, pumpkins, witches).
- Have students put together sets of erasers; match sets with the correct number card. Reverse the activity by placing the erasers in groups according to category (e.g., ghosts, pumpkins, witches), and having the students count and label the sets with number cards. (Number cards are not included.)

## Memory Game

- To make cards, cut out 10 two-inch squares of construction paper.
- Affix five different Halloween stickers on five of the cards. Repeat using the five matching stickers. (There will be five pairs of stickers). Laminate the cards, if desired.

- Mix up the deck and place the cards face down on the table.

- Have one student turn over one card, then another, trying to find a matched pair. If the cards do not match, the student should turn the cards back over for the next student. If a student makes a match, s/he keeps the cards and plays again.

- The object of the game is to collect the most pairs.

- Optional: To extend the game, create more sticker pairs.

## Create the Calendar

# Directions

1. Reproduce each pattern onto the suggested paper (see "Calendar Components").

2. Provide each student with the calendar components, and with your class complete the following steps:

3. Cut out the pattern pieces.

4. Glue the yellow house and moon on the black paper, above the actual calendar.

5. Glue the brown haunted house on top of the yellow haunted house. Be careful not to glue the flaps down.

6. Glue the poem on the black construction paper in the lower left-hand corner.

7. Fold back each flap and make sets inside with fingertips and a black stamp pad. Create the details with a fine-tip felt marker. For example, place three black finger prints inside one window and use the marker to add wings and faces. Inside the door mark five fingerprints and add eight pairs of legs to each. Inside the second window, place three black fingerprints and add pointed hats and faces to create three witches. Inside the attic window, print two finger prints and add jack-o-lantern faces and stems with a pen. (See samples, page 151.)

8. Make ghosts emerging from the chimney by dipping the index finger in white paint. Touch your finger to the paper above the chimney. Pull your finger downward to form a "tail." When the paint has dried, add a face using a black fine-tip felt marker.

## Calendar Components

## Each student will need:

- 1 October Calendar affixed to the bottom half of a 12" x 18" piece of black construction paper

- 1 poem

- 1 moon; 1 haunted house interior (reproduce on yellow paper)

- 1 haunted house exterior (reproduce on brown construction paper)

- access to fine-tip markers, white poster paint, and black stamp pad

## Halloween Surprise

The rafters are creaking,
The hinges are squeaking,
The wind is howling
And dogs are growling;
The windows clatter
(My teeth start to chatter),
Then I hear ring - ring - ring:
"Happy Halloween!"

## Halloween Surprise

The rafters are creaking,
The hinges are squeaking,
The wind is howling
And dogs are growling;
The windows clatter
(My teeth start to chatter),
Then I hear ring - ring - ring:
"Happy Halloween!"

## Halloween Surprise

The rafters are creaking,
The hinges are squeaking,
The wind is howling
And dogs are growling;
The windows clatter
(My teeth start to chatter),
Then I hear ring - ring - ring:
"Happy Halloween!"

## Halloween Surprise

The rafters are creaking,
The hinges are squeaking,
The wind is howling
And dogs are growling;
The windows clatter
(My teeth start to chatter),
Then I hear ring - ring - ring:
"Happy Halloween!"

## Halloween Surprise

The rafters are creaking,
The hinges are squeaking,
The wind is howling
And dogs are growling;
The windows clatter
(My teeth start to chatter),
Then I hear ring - ring - ring:
"Happy Halloween!"

## Halloween Surprise

The rafters are creaking,
The hinges are squeaking,
The wind is howling
And dogs are growling;
The windows clatter
(My teeth start to chatter),
Then I hear ring - ring - ring:
"Happy Halloween!"

— Reproducible Page —

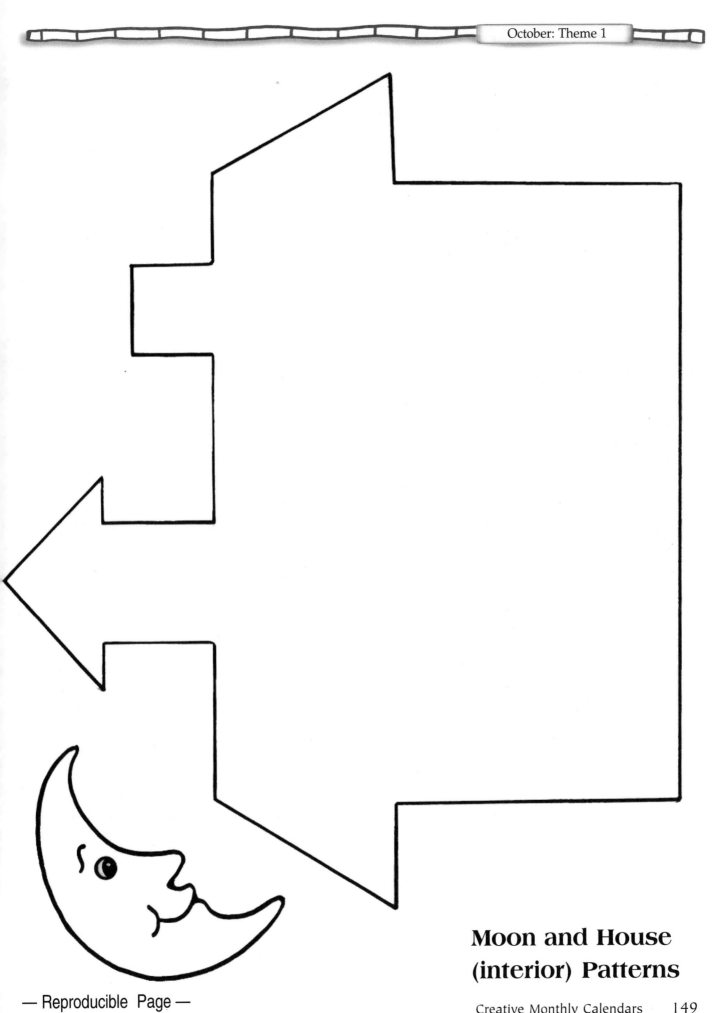

## Moon and House (interior) Patterns

— Reproducible Page —

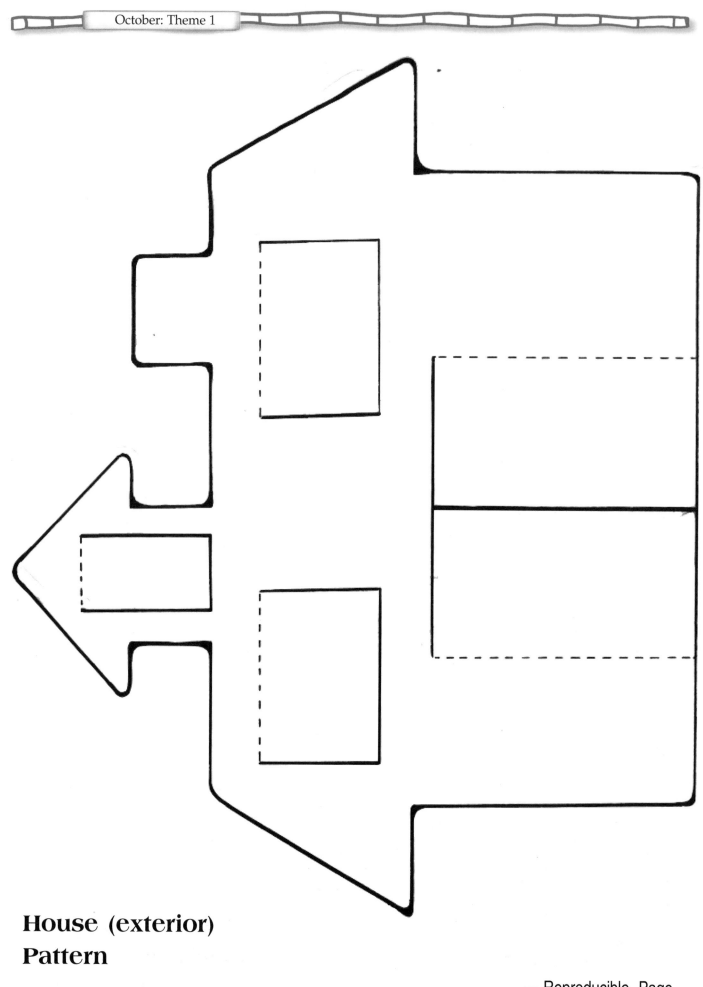

## House (exterior)
## Pattern

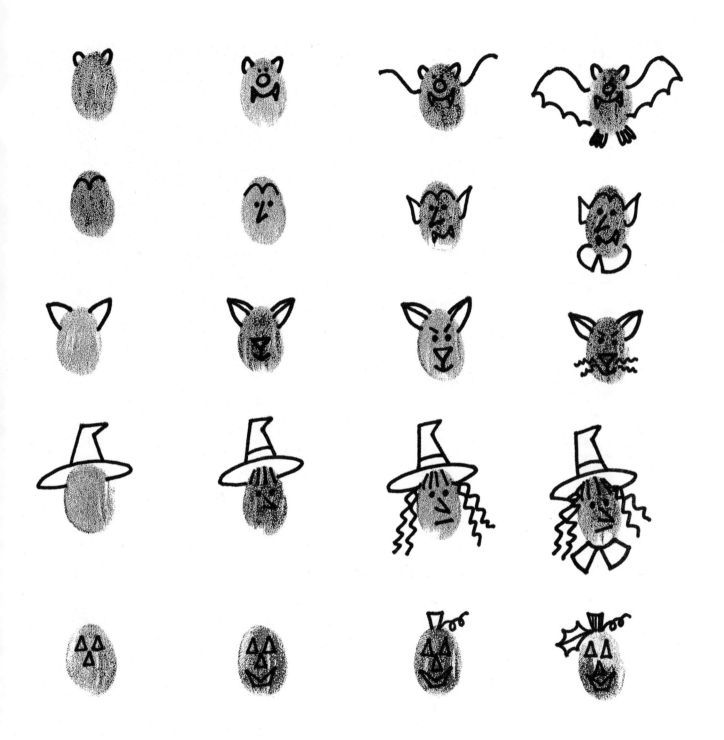

# Thumbprint Pattern How-To's

# Literature LINK

- *Fall Leaves* by Mary Packard
- *Autumn: An Alphabet Acrostic* by Steven Schnur
- *Leaves, Leaves, Leaves* by Nancy Elizabeth Wallace
- *Red Leaf, Yellow Leaf* by Lois Ehlert

## Fall Leaves

Red, yellow, orange, brown,
Fall leaves flutter to the ground,
Leaving branches tall and bare,
A wintry chill is in the air.

## ACTIVITIES ➤

### SKILL CODES

## A, B, C, F, G, I

## Leaf Patterns

- Reproduce the leaf pattern onto paper, various colors. Cut out the patterns and laminate.
- Have students create or extend patterns (by color, type, etc.) using the different colored leaves.
- Introduce more difficult concepts to the patterning such as pointing up or down, left or right.

## Leaf Numbers

- Reproduce the leaf pattern on various autumn-colored papers.
- Write the numerals 0 through 10 (one number per leaf) on the leaf patterns. Cut out and laminate.
- Use the numeral leaves as flash-cards to play number recognition games. You might also have the students place the leaves in numerical order to form a number line.

# Leaf Memory Game

- Make two sets of the numeral leaves and turn them number-side down to play a memory game.
- Taking turns, have each student flip over two leaves at a time. If this player's pairs match, s/he should keep the pair. If the leaves do not match, students should turn the leaves face down again.
- Another student now tries to match two cards.
- The player who has the most pairs at the end of the game is the winner.

## Create the Calendar

# Directions

1. Reproduce each pattern onto the suggested paper (see "Calendar Components").
2. Provide each student with the calendar components, and with your class complete the following steps:
3. Cut out the pattern pieces.
4. Arrange the leaves in a pattern in a circle on the dark-blue construction paper (above the actual calendar). It may be helpful to draw a circle on each child's paper. Glue the leaves onto the paper.
5. Glue the bow at the bottom of the wreath.
6. Glue the acorns on the wreath as an accent.
7. Glue the poem in the center of the wreath.

## Calendar Components

### Each student will need:
- 1 October Calendar affixed to the bottom half of a 12" x 18" piece of dark-blue construction paper
- 1 poem
- 8-10 leaves (reproduce on various "autumn" shades of paper)
- 4-6 acorns (reproduce on tan and/or brown paper)
- 1 bow (reproduce on a piece of colored paper that contrasts leaf colors already selected)

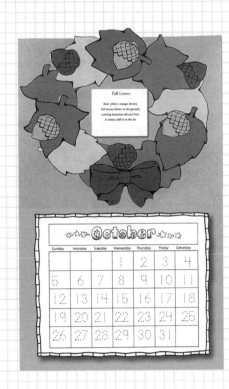

## Fall Leaves

Red, yellow, orange, brown,
Fall leaves flutter to the ground,
Leaving branches tall and bare,
A wintry chill is in the air.

## Fall Leaves

Red, yellow, orange, brown,
Fall leaves flutter to the ground,
Leaving branches tall and bare,
A wintry chill is in the air.

## Fall Leaves

Red, yellow, orange, brown,
Fall leaves flutter to the ground,
Leaving branches tall and bare,
A wintry chill is in the air.

## Fall Leaves

Red, yellow, orange, brown,
Fall leaves flutter to the ground,
Leaving branches tall and bare,
A wintry chill is in the air.

## Fall Leaves

Red, yellow, orange, brown,
Fall leaves flutter to the ground,
Leaving branches tall and bare,
A wintry chill is in the air.

## Fall Leaves

Red, yellow, orange, brown,
Fall leaves flutter to the ground,
Leaving branches tall and bare,
A wintry chill is in the air.

# Leaf Patterns

# Acorn Pattern

— Reproducible  Page —

**Bow Pattern for Wreath**

# Fun Celebrations for October

## October 1

- This is the first day of National Dinosaur Month and National Go on a Fieldtrip Month. Plan a trip to the nearest natural history museum, or discuss what it would be like to work as a paleontologist.

- This is also the first day of Book It! Read Program, sponsored by Pizza Hut. For more information on this reading-incentive program, call (800) 4-Bookit, or visit www.bookitprogram.com.

## October 2

This is National Custodial Workers' Day. Have your students show your custodian how much you appreciate her/him by helping clean up the playground and classroom. Discuss the importance of appreciating and caring for the people, creatures, surroundings, and objects you encounter *every* day.

## October 5

Today is International Frugal Fun day. This is a day to celebrate having fun without spending a lot of money. Host a class picnic and plan group activities such as a relay race or Duck, Duck Goose.

## Second Week of October

This is Fire Prevention Week. Plan a field trip to a fire station or invite a firefighter to your class to discuss fire safety with your students.

## October 7

Marc Brown's popular series featuring Arthur the aardvark and his sister D.W. premiered on television today in 1996. Celebrate by watching an Arthur video or reading an Arthur book.

## October 16

It's National Dictionary Day. Plan a lesson around using dictionaries, and/or have students create their own word-list dictionaries on the computer.

## October 25

Happy Birthday to Pablo Picasso. Introduce your students to contemporary art. Create some contemporary art of your own to celebrate.

## October 31

Happy Halloween! Take a few moments to discuss trick-or-treating safety. Ask each child to share what s/he will be for Halloween. Graph the results.

# November

## Theme 1:
## Thanksgiving

## Theme 2:
## Harvest

# Literature LINK

- *Over the River and Through the Woods* by Lydia Marie Child
- *Thanksgiving Day* by Gail Gibbons
- *A Plump and Perky Turkey* by Teresa Bateman

## Ten Little Turkeys

Ten little turkeys stand in a row,
Tail feathers forming ten rainbows.

Each turkey stands on ten turkey toes;
Each turkey drinks from one turkey bowl.

Scratch, scratch, peck, peck,
Gobble, gobble, gobble;
Ten little turkeys
Waddle, waddle, waddle.

## ACTIVITIES ➤

## SKILL CODES

## A, B, C, H, I, J

## Fraction Fun

- Make a variety of popular foods out of construction paper: pizza, pie, cookies, etc.

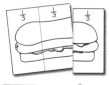

- Cut each item into a different fraction (cut the pizza in half, the pie into fourths, etc.) and laminate.

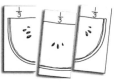

- Use these manipulatives to explore fractions.

- Here's a sample conversation: "If you and I go to a pizza parlor and split a pepperoni pizza, how much pizza will we each be able to eat? We will divide the pizza in half: one-half for you and one-half for me."

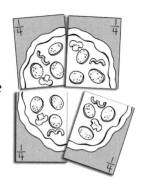

## Nutrition

- Collect a variety of plastic foods for students to use as sorting and classifying manipulatives.

- Make a food pyramid graph out of felt or butcher paper. (Graph should be approximately four-feet tall, although size can depend on the number/size of the items you choose to graph.)

- Lay the graph on the ground and ask students to sort the

food items by food group. You might ask students questions such as: "How many items are in the grain group? How many items are in the fruit group? What common characteristics can be found in each of the food groups?"

# Create the Calendar

# Directions

1. Reproduce each pattern onto the suggested paper (see "Calendar Components").

2. Provide each student with the calendar components, and with your class complete the following steps:

3. Color each turkey beak yellow; color each wattle red; highlight the eyes with a white pencil.

4. Cut out the pattern pieces.

5. Glue the poem on the upper left-hand corner of the page (above the actual calendar).

6. Arrange the turkeys along the bottom edge of the calendar, overlapping patterns as necessary. (Be careful not to cover the poem.)

7. Once students have arranged the turkeys, glue each in place.

## Calendar Components

## Each student will need:
- 1 November Calendar affixed to the bottom half of a 12" x 18" piece of green construction paper
- 1 poem
- 1 sheet of 10 turkeys (reproduce on tan construction paper)
- access to magic markers

## Ten Little Turkeys

Ten little turkeys stand in a row,
Tail feathers forming ten rainbows.

Each turkey stands on ten turkey toes;
Each turkey drinks from one turkey bowl.

Scratch, scratch, peck, peck,
Gobble, gobble, gobble;
Ten little turkeys
Waddle, waddle, waddle.

## Ten Little Turkeys

Ten little turkeys stand in a row,
Tail feathers forming ten rainbows.

Each turkey stands on ten turkey toes;
Each turkey drinks from one turkey bowl.

Scratch, scratch, peck, peck,
Gobble, gobble, gobble;
Ten little turkeys
Waddle, waddle, waddle.

## Ten Little Turkeys

Ten little turkeys stand in a row,
Tail feathers forming ten rainbows.

Each turkey stands on ten turkey toes;
Each turkey drinks from one turkey bowl.

Scratch, scratch, peck, peck,
Gobble, gobble, gobble;
Ten little turkeys
Waddle, waddle, waddle.

## Ten Little Turkeys

Ten little turkeys stand in a row,
Tail feathers forming ten rainbows.

Each turkey stands on ten turkey toes;
Each turkey drinks from one turkey bowl.

Scratch, scratch, peck, peck,
Gobble, gobble, gobble;
Ten little turkeys
Waddle, waddle, waddle.

## Ten Little Turkeys

Ten little turkeys stand in a row,
Tail feathers forming ten rainbows.

Each turkey stands on ten turkey toes;
Each turkey drinks from one turkey bowl.

Scratch, scratch, peck, peck,
Gobble, gobble, gobble;
Ten little turkeys
Waddle, waddle, waddle.

## Ten Little Turkeys

Ten little turkeys stand in a row,
Tail feathers forming ten rainbows.

Each turkey stands on ten turkey toes;
Each turkey drinks from one turkey bowl.

Scratch, scratch, peck, peck,
Gobble, gobble, gobble;
Ten little turkeys
Waddle, waddle, waddle.

## Ten Little Turkeys

Ten little turkeys stand in a row,
Tail feathers forming ten rainbows.

Each turkey stands on ten turkey toes;
Each turkey drinks from one turkey bowl.

Scratch, scratch, peck, peck,
Gobble, gobble, gobble;
Ten little turkeys
Waddle, waddle, waddle.

## Ten Little Turkeys

Ten little turkeys stand in a row,
Tail feathers forming ten rainbows.

Each turkey stands on ten turkey toes;
Each turkey drinks from one turkey bowl.

Scratch, scratch, peck, peck,
Gobble, gobble, gobble;
Ten little turkeys
Waddle, waddle, waddle.

— Reproducible Page —

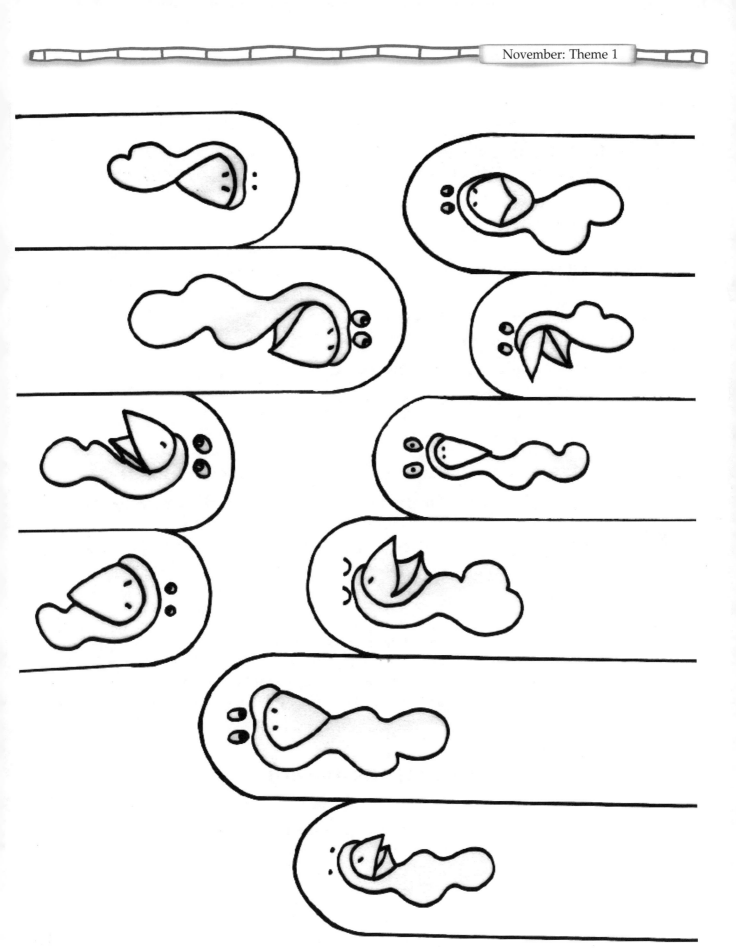

**Turkey Patterns**

# Literature LINK

- *Pumpkin Circle* by George Levenson
- *Pumpkin, Pumpkin* by Jeanne Titherington
- *Apples and Pumpkins* by Anne Rockwell
- *In November* by Cynthia Rylant
- *Pumpkin Day* by Nancy Elizabeth Wallace

## Harvest Time

We gather pumpkins from the ground,
We pick red apples ripe and round,
Squash and nuts and berries too—
A delicious harvest for me and you.

## ACTIVITIES ➤

## SKILL CODES

## A, C, E, H, I, J

## Pumpkin-Compare/Contrast

- Bring in to class a variety of pumpkins (e.g., Munchkin, Orange, and White).
- Sort, order, and classify the pumpkins by type, shape, color, etc. (You can divide them further after the initial sorting.) For instance, you might measure each pumpkin's circumference with a paper strip or yarn by cutting it where one end meets the other. Take the strip/yarn and lay it down on a ruler/ yardstick Have students compare/contrast the different measurements by hanging the strip/yarn pieces next to one another. You might also want to slice a pumpkin in half and measure its diameter. Estimate how many seeds will be inside, and then count the seeds.

## Weight Estimation

- Bring in a scale and a bag of apples.
- Have the students estimate how many apples it will take to equal one pound, two pounds, etc.
- Write down your estimates and then weigh the apples to determine how accurate the estimates are.
- Try the same activity with pumpkins.
- Compare and contrast the apples and pumpkins. How many apples will it take to equal the weight of one pumpkin? How much heavier or lighter is an apple than a pumpkin?

## Create the Calendar

# Directions

1. Reproduce each pattern onto the suggested paper (see "Calendar Components").

2. Provide each student with the calendar components, and with your class complete the following steps:

3. Cut out the pattern pieces.

4. Cut out numerous squares of yellow and orange tissue paper. Set these aside.

5. Under constant adult supervision, have students paint diluted glue (or liquid starch) within the pumpkin shape.

6. Affix the tissue-paper squares on the glue, overlapping and alternating colors until the shape is covered (it is okay for squares to edge off the paper; you and/or students will trim the papers to fit the pumpkin shape once the glue has dried).

7. Paint a layer of glue on top so the tissue paper is thoroughly dampened. Set the pumpkins aside and allow the papers to dry.

8. Reproduce the pumpkin/stem/vine template onto the dark blue construction paper. Affix the blue construction paper to the top portion of the 12" x 18" yellow calendar sheet.

9. Trace each vine segment with glue. Cover the glue with a length of yarn; trim as necessary. Continue until each vine is covered with yarn.

10. Glue a leaf on the end of the vines (not the spirals; see sample calendar).

11. Trim the tissue paper pumpkin. Glue it in place on the blue paper. Add the stem.

12. Glue the poem to the right of the pumpkin, as indicated on the sample calendar.

## Calendar Components

### Each student will need:

- 1 November Calendar affixed to the bottom half of a 12" x 18" piece of yellow construction paper
- 1 poem
- 1 piece of 8½" x 11" dark-blue construction paper
- 1 pumpkin (reproduce on white construction paper)
- orange tissue-paper squares; yellow tissue-paper squares, 1" x 1" (see directions)
- 1 leaf/stem set (reproduce on green paper)
- several strands of green yarn

### Harvest Time

We gather pumpkins from the ground,
We pick red apples ripe and round,
Squash and nuts and berries too—
A delicious harvest for me and you.

### Harvest Time

We gather pumpkins from the ground,
We pick red apples ripe and round,
Squash and nuts and berries too—
A delicious harvest for me and you.

### Harvest Time

We gather pumpkins from the ground,
We pick red apples ripe and round,
Squash and nuts and berries too—
A delicious harvest for me and you.

### Harvest Time

We gather pumpkins from the ground,
We pick red apples ripe and round,
Squash and nuts and berries too—
A delicious harvest for me and you.

### Harvest Time

We gather pumpkins from the ground,
We pick red apples ripe and round,
Squash and nuts and berries too—
A delicious harvest for me and you.

### Harvest Time

We gather pumpkins from the ground,
We pick red apples ripe and round,
Squash and nuts and berries too—
A delicious harvest for me and you.

### Harvest Time

We gather pumpkins from the ground,
We pick red apples ripe and round,
Squash and nuts and berries too—
A delicious harvest for me and you.

### Harvest Time

We gather pumpkins from the ground,
We pick red apples ripe and round,
Squash and nuts and berries too—
A delicious harvest for me and you.

— Reproducible Page —

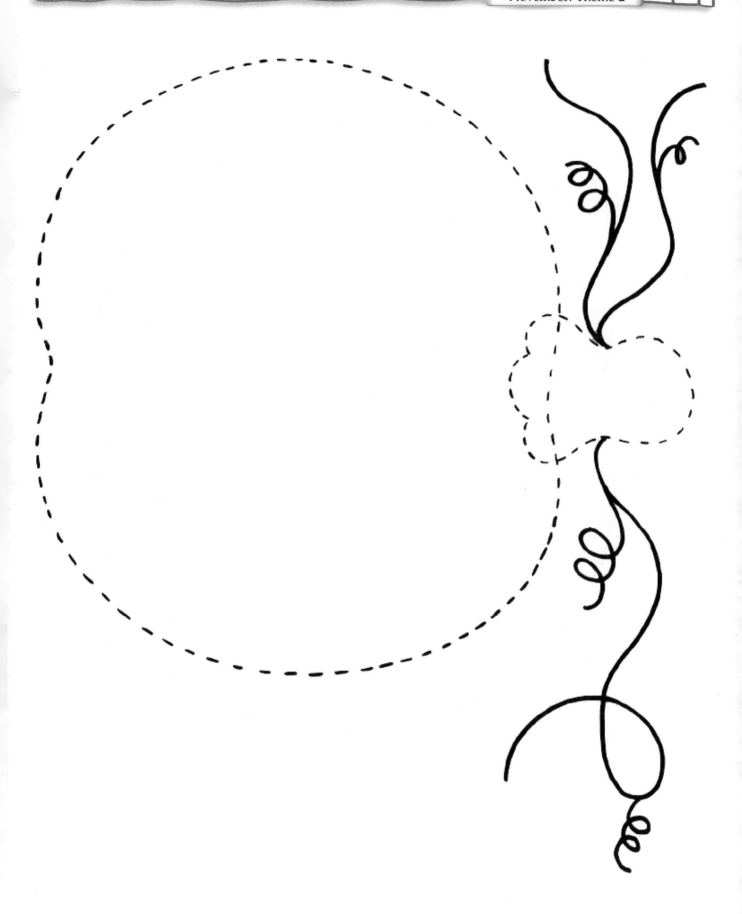

## Pumpkin Template Pattern

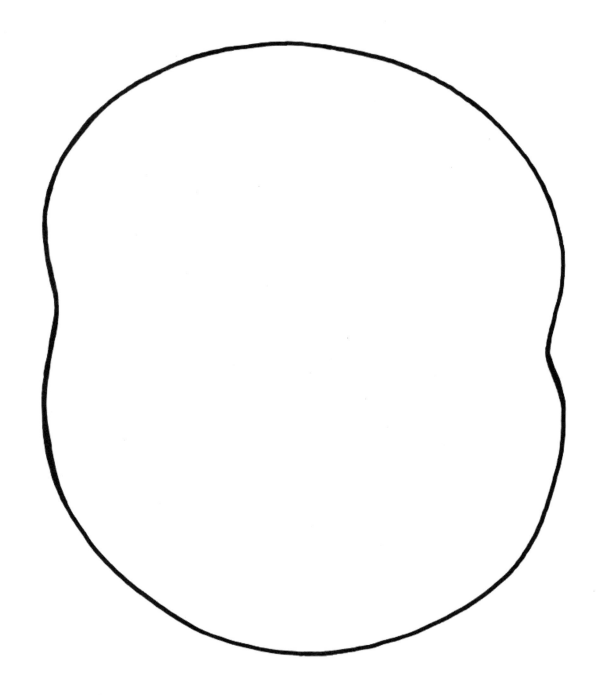

# Pumpkin Pattern

**Leaf Pattern**

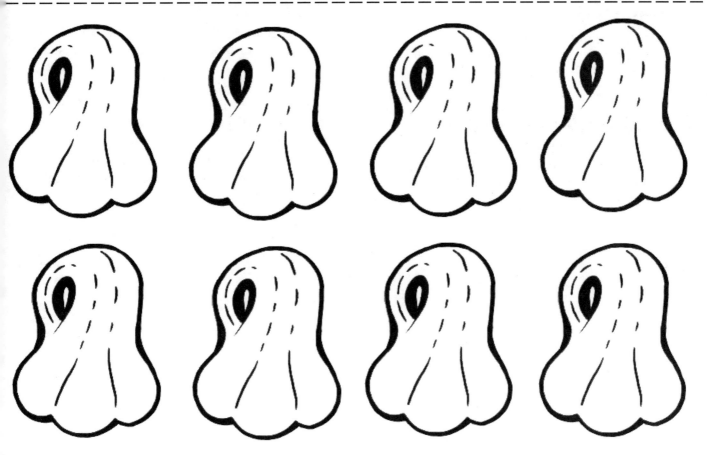

**Stem Pattern**

# Fun Celebrations for November

## First Week of November

This is Kids' Goal Setting Week. See how many books your class can read in one month.

## November 1

- This is National Authors' Day. Encourage your students to write a story of their own and share it with the class. Consider scheduling a visit from a local author today.

- Today is also the first day of National Peanut Butter Lovers' Month. Make several tasty peanut butter treats with your class. Try placing peanut butter on celery, apples, pretzels, or graham crackers. Yum! (Check to make sure no one is allergic to peanuts.)

## November 3

Today is Sandwich Day. Celebrate by having a picnic lunch featuring peanut butter and jelly sandwiches.

## Second Week in November

This is National Parents As Teachers Week. Invite parents to visit the classroom and share a special skill or talent with your students.

## November 6

Today is National Young Readers' Day. Celebrate by having a read-in. Simply set aside time today to read independently or as a group.

## November 10

*Sesame Street* made its television premiere on this day in 1969.

## November 15

This is America Recycles Day. Explain the importance of recycling to your students. Discuss some ways we use recycled materials.

## November 18

- Created on this day in 1902 was the teddy bear. For more information on the history of the teddy bear, read *The Legend of the Teddy Bear* by Frank Murphy.

- Happy Birthday, Mickey Mouse! That's right, Mickey was born on this day in 1928. Wear those mouse ears with pride!

- This is What Do You Love About America Day. Have your students share three things they love about our country.

# December

## Theme 1:
## Gingerbread

## Theme 2:
## Gift-Giving

# Literature LINK

- *The Gingerbread Baby* by Jan Brett
- *Cajun Gingerbread Boy* by Berthe Amoss
- *The Gingerbread Man* by Pam Adams

## Gingerbread*

Six little gingerbread boys lying on a tray—
One jumped up and ran away.
Five little gingerbread boys lined up in a row—
One jumped up and away did go.
Four little gingerbread boys (still piping hot!)—
One jumped up and left at a trot.
Three little gingerbread boys cooked golden brown—
One jumped up and leaped to the ground.
Two little gingerbread boys, decorations bright—
One jumped up and skittered out of sight.
One little gingerbread boy decided to run—
He jumped up, and then there were none!

## ACTIVITIES ➤

### SKILL CODES

## A, C, E, G, I, J

## Gingerbread Puzzle

- Color, laminate, and cut out several gingerbread boy patterns.
- Cut each pattern apart into puzzle pieces and store the pieces in a Ziploc bag. For preschoolers, each puzzle should contain four pieces. For older/ more advanced students, make the puzzle more challenging by cutting the patterns into additional pieces.
- Give each child one puzzle bag and ask her/him to put the gingerbread boy back together again.

## Estimation

- Give each student one gingerbread boy pattern and a cup of gumdrops.
- Ask students to estimate how many gumdrops it will take to fill in the gingerbread boy.
- Fill in the gingerbread boy and then count how many gumdrops were used.
- If you have time, bake actual gingerbread cookies with your students (or bake them ahead of time and bring them into class). Decorate, eat, and enjoy!

* Finger-Play

## Create the Calendar

# Directions

1. Reproduce each pattern onto the suggested paper (see "Calendar Components").

2. Provide each student with the calendar components, and with your class complete the following steps:

3. Cut out the pattern pieces.

4. Create a pattern with the candy cane stripes by coloring red-white-red-white or red-white-green, red-white-green.

5. Cut around the outside of the frame. Do not cut the inside edge.

6. Glue the frame in place.

7. Cut out the gingerbread man; decorate. (Have several samples on display to generate decorating ideas for the students.)

8. Glue the completed gingerbread boy inside the frame. Glue the poem next to him.

9. Provide each student with a length of yarn or ribbon to tie a bow, or use the bow pattern on page 177.

## Calendar Components

### Each student will need:
- 1 December Calendar affixed to the bottom of a 12" x 18" piece of green construction paper
- 1 poem
- 1 candy cane frame (reproduce on white paper)
- red marker and/or green marker
- one gingerbread boy (reproduce on tan construction paper)
- materials to decorate gingerbread pattern (e.g., glitter glue, markers, sequins, buttons, stickers, ribbon)

## Gingerbread

Six little gingerbread boys lying on a tray—
    One jumped up and ran away.
Five little gingerbread boys lined up in a row—
    One jumped up and away did go.
Four little gingerbread boys (still piping hot!)—
    One jumped up and left at a trot.
Three little gingerbread boys cooked golden brown—
    One jumped up and leaped to the ground.
Two little gingerbread boys, decorations bright—
    One jumped up and skittered out of sight.
One little gingerbread boy decided to run—
    He jumped up, and then there were none!

## Gingerbread

Six little gingerbread boys lying on a tray—
    One jumped up and ran away.
Five little gingerbread boys lined up in a row—
    One jumped up and away did go.
Four little gingerbread boys (still piping hot!)—
    One jumped up and left at a trot.
Three little gingerbread boys cooked golden brown—
    One jumped up and leaped to the ground.
Two little gingerbread boys, decorations bright—
    One jumped up and skittered out of sight.
One little gingerbread boy decided to run—
    He jumped up, and then there were none!

## Gingerbread

Six little gingerbread boys lying on a tray—
    One jumped up and ran away.
Five little gingerbread boys lined up in a row—
    One jumped up and away did go.
Four little gingerbread boys (still piping hot!)—
    One jumped up and left at a trot.
Three little gingerbread boys cooked golden brown—
    One jumped up and leaped to the ground.
Two little gingerbread boys, decorations bright—
    One jumped up and skittered out of sight.
One little gingerbread boy decided to run—
    He jumped up, and then there were none!

## Gingerbread

Six little gingerbread boys lying on a tray—
    One jumped up and ran away.
Five little gingerbread boys lined up in a row—
    One jumped up and away did go.
Four little gingerbread boys (still piping hot!)—
    One jumped up and left at a trot.
Three little gingerbread boys cooked golden brown—
    One jumped up and leaped to the ground.
Two little gingerbread boys, decorations bright—
    One jumped up and skittered out of sight.
One little gingerbread boy decided to run—
    He jumped up, and then there were none!

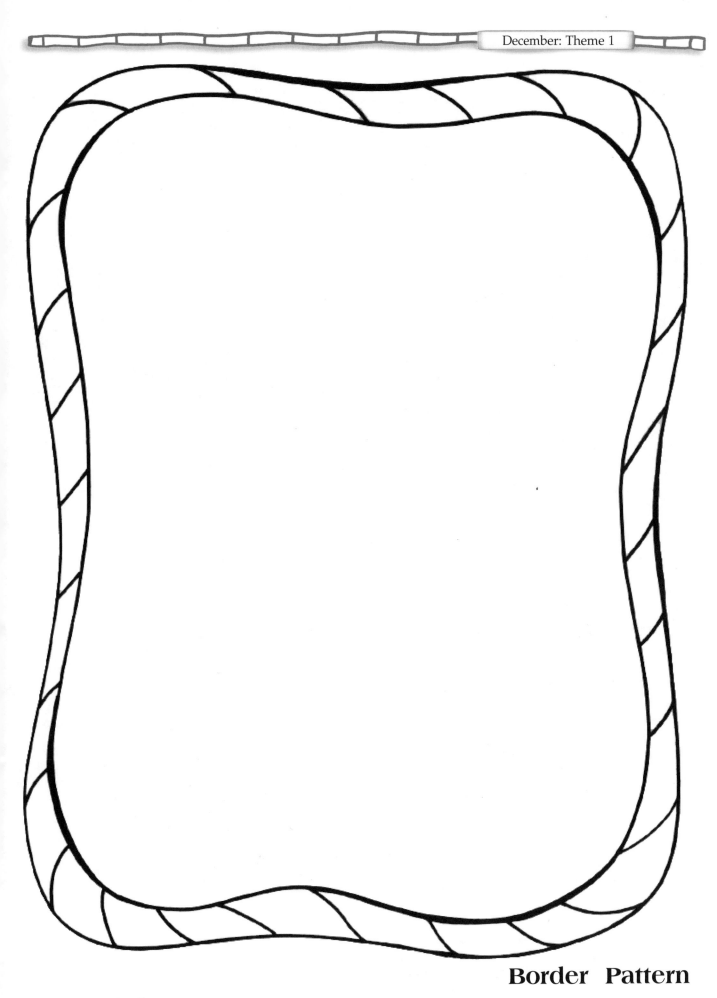

December: Theme 1

**Border Pattern**

# Gingerbread Boy Pattern

— Reproducible  Page —

## Bow Pattern

# Literature LINK

- *Gifts* by Phyllis Limbacher Tildes
- *Lucy's Christmas* by Donald Hall
- *The Gift* by Gabriela Keselman

## Gift-Giving

It's that special time of year
When gifts suddenly appear,
Brightly wrapped and tied with ribbon,
From our loved ones they are given.
Now, I'm sure there's one for you,
(You've been good, I know it's true),
And there must be one for me;
Let's go look under the tree!

## ACTIVITIES ➤

### SKILL CODES

## A, C, D, F, I, J

## Gift Facts

- Reproduce the gift cards onto pieces of different-colored construction paper; cut each pattern out.
- On each card, write an addition or subtraction statement; laminate (just include the statement; do not include the answer).
- Hold a flashcard up in front of the group and ask them to tell you the answer to the fact on the flashcard. See who can guess the answer the quickest.
- Make this into a game by asking two children to stand up at one time. The player who guesses the answer the fastest gets to try again with a new player. This continues on until someone else guesses the answer faster. The winner is the person who answers the most facts correctly in succession.
- If students use this as an independent activity, direct them to write their answers to the equations on a piece of paper for you to check at a later time.

## Gift Game

- Bring in a large gift box with a removable lid.
- Wrap the box and the lid. Add a bow on the top.
- Fill the box with an assortment of recognizable items.

(Focus on geometric shapes such as a clock shaped like a cube, a ball/sphere, a birthday hat/cone, etc.)

- Tell your students you have a package filled with special gifts, but you need their help with identifying each one. Start by giving basic descriptions; provide additional details until students are able to guess correctly. For example, you might say:

   "There is something in my box that is a sphere.
   Can you guess what it might be?
   This sphere is made of rubber.
   Any guesses yet?
   You're right, it's a ball!"

- You might choose to give each student a small gift, such as a sticker or a gummy bear, when the activity is complete.

## Create the Calendar

# Directions

1. Provide each student with the calendar components, and with your class complete the following steps:

2. On the white construction paper piece ask students to draw three to four items they would like to give or receive as gifts. For younger students you might encourage them to brainstorm ideas out loud; write down their choices. Or use the optional gift patterns that the students have colored in.

3. After students have finished drawing and coloring, have them cut the items out and arrange them on the calendar as if they are inside the wrapping paper box, as indicated in the sample calendar. After they have arranged their gift items, they should glue them in place.

4. For extra sparkle, add curled ribbon to the package, or add a ribbon border around the outside edges of the calendar.

5. Glue the poem in the upper right-hand corner of the calendar page.

## Calendar Components

### Each student will need:

- 1 December Calendar affixed to the bottom half of a 12" x 18" piece of construction paper (any color may be used to complement the wrapping paper, should you choose this option)
- 1 poem
- 1 piece of wrapping paper (4" x 8" rectangle; you may substitute wrapping paper with colored construction paper if wrapping paper is not available)
- white construction paper (see directions)
- ribbon (curled and/or straight)
- optional gift patterns

## Gift-Giving

It's that special time of year
When gifts suddenly appear,
Brightly wrapped and tied with ribbon,
From our loved ones they are given.
Now, I'm sure there's one for you,
(You've been good, I know it's true),
And there must be one for me;
Let's go look under the tree!

## Gift-Giving

It's that special time of year
When gifts suddenly appear,
Brightly wrapped and tied with ribbon,
From our loved ones they are given.
Now, I'm sure there's one for you,
(You've been good, I know it's true),
And there must be one for me;
Let's go look under the tree!

## Gift-Giving

It's that special time of year
When gifts suddenly appear,
Brightly wrapped and tied with ribbon,
From our loved ones they are given.
Now, I'm sure there's one for you,
(You've been good, I know it's true),
And there must be one for me;
Let's go look under the tree!

## Gift-Giving

It's that special time of year
When gifts suddenly appear,
Brightly wrapped and tied with ribbon,
From our loved ones they are given.
Now, I'm sure there's one for you,
(You've been good, I know it's true),
And there must be one for me;
Let's go look under the tree!

## Gift-Giving

It's that special time of year
When gifts suddenly appear,
Brightly wrapped and tied with ribbon,
From our loved ones they are given.
Now, I'm sure there's one for you,
(You've been good, I know it's true),
And there must be one for me;
Let's go look under the tree!

## Gift-Giving

It's that special time of year
When gifts suddenly appear,
Brightly wrapped and tied with ribbon,
From our loved ones they are given.
Now, I'm sure there's one for you,
(You've been good, I know it's true),
And there must be one for me;
Let's go look under the tree!

## Optional Gift Patterns

# Gift Fact-Card Patterns

— Reproducible  Page —

# Gift Fact-Card Patterns

# Fun Celebrations for December

## December 1

This is the first day of National Bingo Month. Set aside some time in December to play an educational bingo game or two. Such games are available at most teacher supply stores.

## December 2

French painter Georges Seurat was born on this day in 1859. Seurat was well known for his pointillist style of painting, a technique in which the artist renders her/his work in dots. With your students, create your own pointillist piece of artwork (eraser tips dipped in paint work well).

## Second Week in December

This is Tell Someone They're Doing a Good Job Week. What a perfect day to let your students know you are proud of their efforts.

## December 9

The first Christmas cards were created on this day in England in 1842. Have your students make holiday cards to give to their upper-grade buddies or the class next door. Notice and discuss the ways in which your students help to keep the peace in your classroom and on the playground.

## December 10

Dr. Martin Luther King Jr. received the Nobel Peace Prize on this day in 1964.

## December 16

Happy Birthday, Ludwig van Beethoven. This German composer was born on this day in 1770.

## December 21

On this day in 1620 the Pilgrims landed in Plymouth, Massachusetts.

## December 25

Merry Christmas! This is the day many children are visited by Santa Claus. As legend goes, if boys and girls have been nice they will receive presents, but if they have been naughty they will receive only a lump of coal. Discuss this and other issues surrounding this important holiday.

## December 31

This is You're All Done Day and Make Up Your Mind Day. It is a wonderful time to explain to your students that our year is at its end (reflect back on all that they have learned) and that they will need to make up their minds about what to choose for their New Year's resolutions.

# Appendix

| Sunday | Monday | Tuesday | Wednesday | Thursday | Friday | Saturday |
|--------|--------|---------|-----------|----------|--------|----------|
|        |        |         |           |          |        |          |
|        |        |         |           |          |        |          |
|        |        |         |           |          |        |          |
|        |        |         |           |          |        |          |
|        |        |         |           |          |        |          |

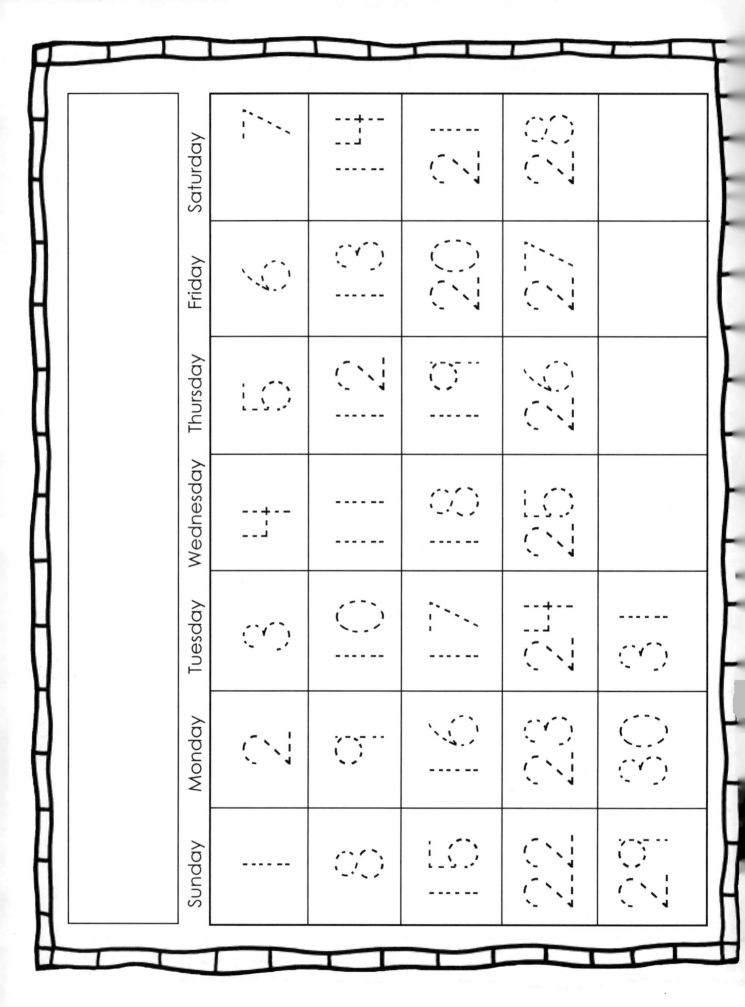

| | Sunday | Monday | Tuesday | Wednesday | Thursday | Friday | Saturday |
|---|---|---|---|---|---|---|---|
| | 1 | 2 | 3 | 4 | 5 | 6 | 7 |
| | 8 | 9 | 10 | 11 | 12 | 13 | 14 |
| | 15 | 16 | 17 | 18 | 19 | 20 | 21 |
| | 22 | 23 | 24 | 25 | 26 | 27 | 28 |
| | 29 | 30 | 31 | | | | |

| Sunday | Monday | Tuesday | Wednesday | Thursday | Friday | Saturday |
|--------|--------|---------|-----------|----------|--------|----------|
|  | 1 | 2 | 3 | 4 | 5 | 6 |
| 7 | 8 | 9 | 10 | 11 | 12 | 13 |
| 14 | 15 | 16 | 17 | 18 | 19 | 20 |
| 21 | 22 | 23 | 24 | 25 | 26 | 27 |
| 28 | 29 | 30 | 31 |  |  |  |

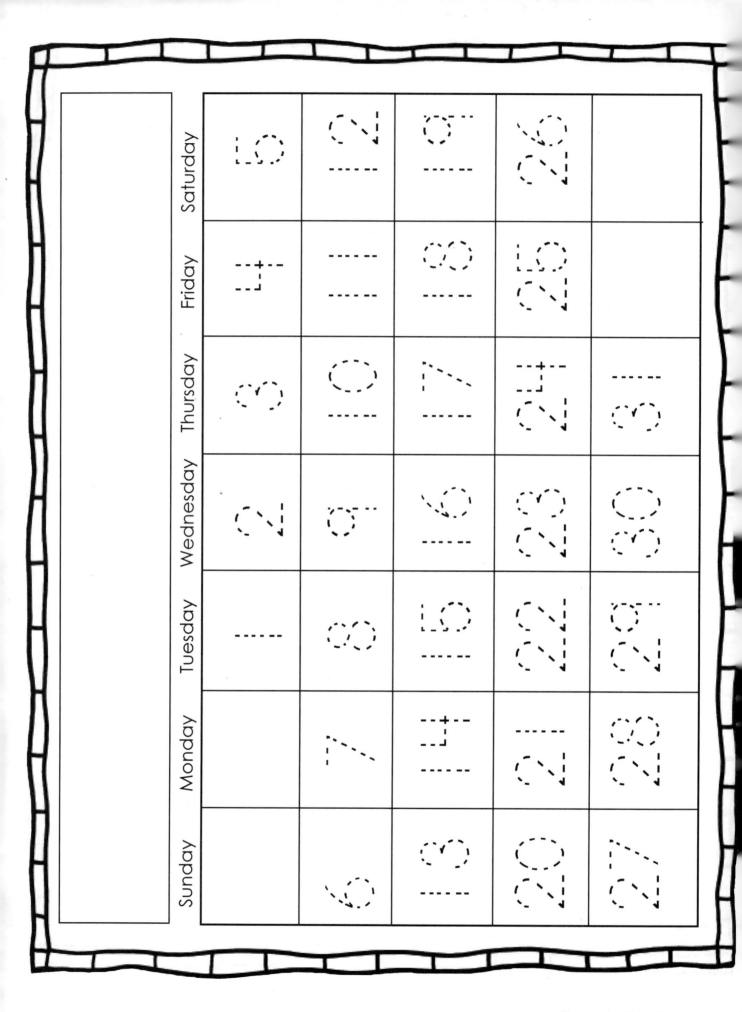

— Reproducible Page —

| Sunday | Monday | Tuesday | Wednesday | Thursday | Friday | Saturday |
|---|---|---|---|---|---|---|
|  |  |  | 1 | 2 | 3 | 4 |
| 5 | 6 | 7 | 8 | 9 | 10 | 11 |
| 12 | 13 | 14 | 15 | 16 | 17 | 18 |
| 19 | 20 | 21 | 22 | 23 | 24 | 25 |
| 26 | 27 | 28 | 29 | 30 | 31 |  |

| Sunday | Monday | Tuesday | Wednesday | Thursday | Friday | Saturday |
|---|---|---|---|---|---|---|
|  |  |  |  | 1 | 2 | 3 |
| 4 | 5 | 6 | 7 | 8 | 9 | 10 |
| 11 | 12 | 13 | 14 | 15 | 16 | 17 |
| 18 | 19 | 20 | 21 | 22 | 23 | 24 |
| 25 | 26 | 27 | 28 | 29 | 30 | 31 |

— Reproducible Page —

| Sunday | Monday | Tuesday | Wednesday | Thursday | Friday | Saturday |
|---|---|---|---|---|---|---|
|  |  |  |  |  | 1 | 2 |
| 3 | 4 | 5 | 6 | 7 | 8 | 9 |
| 10 | 11 | 12 | 13 | 14 | 15 | 16 |
| 17 | 18 | 19 | 20 | 21 | 22 | 23 |
| 24 | 25 | 26 | 27 | 28 | 29 | 30 |
| 31 |  |  |  |  |  |  |

| Sunday | Monday | Tuesday | Wednesday | Thursday | Friday | Saturday |
|--------|--------|---------|-----------|----------|--------|----------|
|   |   |   |   |   |   | 1 |
| 2 | 3 | 4 | 5 | 6 | 7 | 8 |
| 9 | 10 | 11 | 12 | 13 | 14 | 15 |
| 16 | 17 | 18 | 19 | 20 | 21 | 22 |
| 23 | 24 | 25 | 26 | 27 | 28 | 29 |
| 30 | 31 |   |   |   |   |   |

— Reproducible Page —